THE ART OF
ELEGANCE

How to Elevate Your Life with Style and Grace

GINA JUDY

The Art of Elegance: How to Elevate Your Life with Style and Grace
© Gina Judy

All rights reserved. This book or any portion thereof may not be reproduced or used in any manner whatsoever without the express written permission of the publisher except for the use of brief quotations in a book review.

ISBN: 979-8-35098-398-2

DEDICATION

To my daughters, Frankie and Sammi, your unique perspectives have enriched my life, and your unwavering love has been a source of strength throughout this process. The bond we share is a treasure, and I hope this book reflects the love and lessons we've cultivated together.

This work is dedicated to you both, with the hope that it may inspire you, as you have inspired me. I am so proud to be your mother, and I look forward to continuing the journey of growth and discovery together.

PREFACE

In a fast-paced world focused on immediate satisfaction and always chasing the next trend, elegance may seem outdated. However, as we uncover its true meaning, we see that it goes beyond passing fads and changing norms. Elegance is not just about style or surface appeal; it embodies a sophisticated mindset, a polished way of living, and a dedication to grace in every aspect of life.

This book, "The Art of Elegance: How to Elevate Your Life with Style and Grace" invites readers to discover the timeless charm of elegance, tracing its origins and examining its significance in modern culture. It serves as a handbook for individuals looking to elevate their fashion sense, develop a sophisticated demeanor, and embrace a purposeful way of life.

In these pages, you'll find captivating stories of people who exemplify elegance in their lives. We'll delve into the secrets behind their charm, poise, and lasting influence on the world. Discover the subtleties of etiquette and social graces, the beauty of fashion and self-presentation, and the significance of living with mindfulness and purpose.

Join me on this journey of discovery as we unravel the timeless appeal of elegance and unlock its power to transform both our inner and outer worlds.

CONTENTS

INTRODUCTION..1

1. THE ESSENCE OF ELEGANCE...5

2. THE ALLURE OF ELEGANCE..11

3. THE LANGUAGE OF ELEGANCE....................................23

4. THE ART OF SELF PRESENTATION..........................41

5. TIMELESS STYLE AND FASHION...............................87

6. THE ELEGANCE OF A SIGNATURE SCENT......129

7. THE ELEGANCE OF LIVING..145

8. CULTIVATING AN ELEGANT LIFESTYLE..........177

9. ELEGANT SHOPPING...197

10. ICONS OF ELEGANCE..205

11. ACHIEVING ELEGANCE..217

12. AN ELEGANT YOU...229

13. ENDINGS AND BEGINNINGS................................239

14. ANSWERING YOUR QUESTIONS........................247

INTRODUCTION

Welcome to "The Art of Elegance," a heartfelt guide to living your best life with style and grace. In our fast-paced world, where trends come and go at the blink of an eye, the essence of elegance often feels elusive. Yet, elegance is not merely about the clothes we wear or the possessions we accumulate; it is a way of being that transcends the superficial and resonates deeply within our hearts and minds.

This book is an invitation to rediscover the beauty of simplicity, authenticity, and intentionality in our daily lives. It is a celebration of the small, meaningful choices that elevate our everyday experiences and encapsulate the art of living well. Here, you will find insights and inspiration across a spectrum of topics-from cultivating a timeless wardrobe and creating a serene home environment to nurturing relationships that enrich our lives and embracing a mindset of gratitude and mindfulness.

Each chapter is designed to offer practical advice and thoughtful reflections that empower you to cultivate elegance in all its forms. You will learn how to infuse grace into your interactions, develop a personal style that reflects your unique essence, and create an atmosphere of warmth and beauty wherever you go.

Elegance is not about perfection; it is about authenticity and the grace with which we navigate the complexities of life.

As you embark on this journey through the pages of "The Art of Elegance," I encourage you to embrace the transformative power of small changes. Let this book serve as your companion and mentor, guiding you to uncover the elegance that lies within you and inspiring you to live a life that is not only stylish but also deeply fulfilling.

So, if you are ready to embark on this journey of self-discovery and elegance, I invite you to turn the page and step into a world where your best life awaits – one that is infused with style, grace, and, above all, authenticity. Let's begin this adventure together and unlock the extraordinary potential within you.

The journey begins now.

"Elegance is a lifestyle, a state of mind, a delicate balance of poise and grace."

– Gina Judy

1

THE ESSENCE OF ELEGANCE

In a world where fashion and trends dictate social currency, I believe it's time to uncover the true essence of elegance. It's not just about the clothes we wear or the superficial exterior we present to the world. No, elegance is a force that emanates from within, an aura that surrounds those who embody it. It's a way of life, a mindset, a delicate balance of poise and grace.

Imagine a grand ballroom filled with people donned in the latest haute couture, their outward appearances impeccable. Yet, there is one individual who captures your attention, not because they are loud or attention-seeking, but because they exude a quiet confidence. Their movements are graceful, their words carry weight, and their presence fills the room with a sense of calm power. This person embodies the true essence of elegance, a refined spirit that transcends the superficial and fleeting.

Elegance, as I see it, is not about achieving perfection; it's about embracing the process of self-discovery and refinement, finding joy in the journey itself. It's about cultivating a mindset of grace, embracing the pleasures of life, and extending kindness and respect to those around us. It's about recognizing that true elegance is not about keeping up with the latest trends but about discovering our unique inner light and letting it shine through, illuminating the world around us with a soft, radiant glow.

Imagine a ballet dancer effortlessly gliding across the stage, or a diplomat confidently navigating a complex event. Both exude an elegance that comes from years of dedication and practice. But elegance is not just about physical grace. It is a state of inner ease and harmony that allows one to handle life's challenges with poise and composure. It is about moving through the world with a gentle, unhurried grace, emanating a sense of tranquility and inner strength.

Refinement involves cultivating a refined taste and appreciation for life's finer things. It requires understanding social nuances and having a refined palate for physical and intellectual experiences. Actively seeking beauty and engaging in enriching dialogue are essential for refinement.

The concept of elegance, like a fine wine, has aged beautifully, its essence evolving through the centuries. To understand elegance, one must trace its journey, from the grand gestures of ancient civilizations to the subtle nuances of the modern era.

Throughout history, elegance has been intertwined with ideals of beauty, balance, and harmony. From ancient Greece and Rome, where statues like the Venus de Milo and Apollo Belvedere set standards of physical perfection, to the opulent lifestyles of the Romans reflected in their architecture, clothing, and gatherings, elegance has influenced art and culture for centuries. The Middle Ages added a spiritual dimension to elegance through courtly love and intricate art, while the Renaissance saw a renewed focus on individual beauty and perfection.

The 18th century was known as the "Golden Age of Elegance," with a focus on pleasure and refinement in European society. The Industrial Revolution brought a shift in the concept of elegance, with the emerging middle class embracing practicality and challenging traditional norms. Today, elegance continues to evolve, but its essence remains the same – a pursuit of beauty, grace, and refinement.

The 20th century witnessed a dramatic evolution in the concept of elegance, influenced by war, social upheaval, and technological advances. The roaring twenties brought a sense of liberation and rebellion against Victorian constraints, with flapper dresses, bobbed haircuts, and a more relaxed approach to social behavior. The rise of fashion designers like Coco Chanel and Elsa Schiaparelli further challenged traditional notions of elegance, embracing minimalist lines, functional fabrics, and a focus on comfort and practicality.

The renowned designer, Coco Chanel, possessed an unparallelled sense of elegance. Her designs were characterized by simplicity, sophistication and a focus on clean lines and impeccable tailoring. One of Chanel's most iconic creations is the little black dress, a timeless and versatile garment that has become a staple in every well-dressed woman's wardrobe – and one of the inspirations for the title and content of this book. The elegance of Coco Chanel lies in her ability to create effortlessly chic and sophisticated designs that have stood the test of time.

Elsa Schiaparelli was a fashion designer who brought a sense of sophistication and refinement to the world of fashion. Despite her avant-garde and often whimsical designs, Schiaparelli had a keen eye for tailoring and craftsmanship that set her apart from her contemporaries.

Her designs were known for their intricate detailing, exquisite construction, and mastery of the art of dressmaking. Schiaparelli was also known for her innovative use of materials, such as incorporating zippers, cellophane, and other unusual fabrics into her designs. Schiaparelli's sophistication was also evident in her ability to blend the works of art and fashion seamlessly. She collaborated with artists, such as Salvador Dali and Jean Cocteau, creating pieces that were truly works of art in their own right.

Overall, the elegance and sophistication of Elsa Schiaparelli can be seen in her attention to detail, her impeccable craftsmanship, and her ability to seamlessly merge the worlds of art and fashion.

Both Chanel and Schiaparelli continue to be celebrated for their elegance and timeless appeal, making them true icons of sophistication and elegance in the world of fashion.

In the mid-20th century, the rise of mid-century modern design, with its focus on clean lines, functional furniture, and minimalist aesthetics, influenced the perception of elegance. The iconic designs of architects like Mies van der Rohe and Le Corbusier, with their emphasis on simplicity and functionality, redefined the notion of sophistication.

The latter half of the 20th century saw a further blurring of lines between traditional elegance and contemporary styles. Designers like Oscar de la Renta and Ralph Lauren captured the essence of elegance, luxury, and a more inclusive understanding of understated refinement.

Known for his luxurious and feminine designs, Oscar de la Renta, was a master of elegance and glamour. His evening gowns and cocktail dresses were favored by high-profile clients and celebrities for their timeless and sophisticated appeal.

American fashion designer, Ralph Lauren, is synonymous with classic American style and sophistication. His preppy, yet elegant designs, which often feature tailored suits, cashmere sweaters, and flowing evening gowns, capture the essence of understated luxury.

As we enter the 21st century, elegance continues to evolve, adapting to the demands of a rapidly changing world. While the traditional values of grace, sophistication, and refinement remain relevant, contemporary elegance embraces a more relaxed approach to style.

By exploring the descriptors of what is perceived as elegant over time, we gain a deeper appreciation of what constitutes elegance – and we can identify the elements of elegance.

Whether we are describing elegance in architecture, fashion, or a dinner party – we tend to use terms like "refinement", "sophistication", "timeless", and "stylish". "Effortless" and "understated" also seem to appear.

As we have seen in this Chapter, elegance is not a static concept, it is a concept that has evolved over time. We have also noted similarities in the descriptions of what is perceived as elegant.

As we delve into the past, our understanding of elegance grows, and we come to truly recognize its lasting influence. In the upcoming chapter, we will examine the potency of elegance through a research-based perspective.

"The power of elegance lies in its ability to captivate and promise the extraordinary."
– Gina Judy"

2

THE ALLURE OF ELEGANCE

It was at the Cafe de Paris in Monte-Carlo when I saw her. She was the epitome of elegance. With her impeccable straight hair and striking features, she exuded captivating sophistication. Clad in a fitted black dress and simple classic pumps, she moved with grace and poise, each step a dance of confidence and allure. A hint of gold around her wrist caught my eye and I wondered if it was a luxurious link bracelet or possibly a slender Cartier watch with a few diamond accents. When she placed her structured handbag on the small stool next to her chair, I noticed the touch of gold on the bag coordinated beautifully with the glitz of jewelry that caught the eye.

And just as I had done when she first entered, I noticed others turning to capture a glimpse of her. It wasn't just her physical appearance, but also her aura of sophistication and refinement. She had a way of making even the simplest of actions seem elegant – from sipping her wine to closing her menu. Her allure went beyond her appearance and mannerisms. It was in the way she carried herself, with a quiet confidence that demanded respect.

Periodically she spoke with a member of the wait staff, but it would be impossible to hear what she said unless you were extremely close. I imagined her voice was velvety, each word carefully chosen and delivered with perhaps a hint of mystery.

There was purpose in her poise, as if she knew something that others didn't. There was something about her that made people want to see and witness her, to perhaps bask in her elegant presence. It was as if she was magnetized, effortlessly drawing others in with her allure. And in a world where elegance is often overlooked, she stood out like a rare and precious gem, captivating those who crossed her path.

And there it was observed . . . the power of elegance. The power to transform the mundane into moments of beauty . . . to seek the sublime in every day.

The power of elegance lies in its ability to captivate and promise the extraordinary, inviting those who encounter it to embrace beauty and grace in their lives. It carries a certain type of allure and appeal. It draws others in . . . often in a powerful way.

This allure can be attributed to a combination of physical, psychological, and cultural factors that create a captivating presence.

Elegance and Happiness

While the link between elegance and happiness is subjective and varies from person to person, social research and studies in psychology suggest there is a connection between how individuals present themselves, how they are perceived by others, and their overall well-being.

In some cultures, elegance and sophistication are associated with a higher social status. A higher social status tends to lead to increased opportunities and social support. When individuals have access to new experiences and a supportive network, they often feel encouraged to pursue their goals, which can lead to a greater sense of purpose and fulfillment. Access to opportunities – whether in education, employment, or personal development – can lead to improvements in quality of life. When people feel they have the means to pursue their interests and passions, their overall feelings of satisfaction and happiness tend to increase.

In terms of self-expression and confidence, individuals who are perceived as elegant often show confidence in their appearance and demeanor. Research shows that self-confidence can correlate with higher levels of joy and life satisfaction. When individuals feel that they are presenting themselves in a way that resonates with their identity, it can enhance their mood and lead to a greater level of happiness.

Studies in social psychology show that people who are perceived positively by others (including attributes like elegance) tend to experience better social interactions and relationships. Social acceptance and admiration can boost an individual's confidence and overall mood. In this spirit positive social interactions and relationships are linked to increased satisfaction. People who are perceived as elegant tend to receive positive social feedback, this positive feedback elevates their feelings of happiness.

According to research, first impressions are formed quickly and can be influenced by a person's appearance, including their perceived level of elegance. Positive first impressions tend to lead to more favorable social experiences, which can contribute to a greater sense of satisfaction and feelings of happiness.

Likewise, research in the field of aesthetics suggest that individuals who appreciate beauty and aesthetics, which can include elegance in design, fashion, and art, may experience a greater sense of happiness. This appreciation of elegance enhances an individual's level of life satisfaction and emotional well-being.

Finally, engaging in the practice of elegance often involves mindfulness—being present and attentive to one's surroundings and behavior. Mindfulness practices have been associated with improved mental health, reduced stress, and increased happiness. An elegant approach to life often requires mindfulness and attention to detail, which can lead to more present and fulfilling experiences. Such mindfulness can contribute to greater happiness.

While happiness is subjective and can be influenced by a multitude of factors, including personal circumstances, achievements, relationships, and a sense of purpose, social research and studies in psychology point to a connection between perceived elegance and happiness.

To further illustrate this connection, let's take a closer look at how elegance influences perceptions.

The Halo Effect

Elegance often makes a strong first impression. People tend to perceive elegantly dressed individuals as more attractive, which can lead to positive biases. For example, during a job interview, a candidate who presents themselves elegantly may be viewed as more professional and intelligent right from the start.

Why does this phenomenon take place?

A closer look at the research in psychology and sociology may shed light on the allure of elegance and how it influences perceptions.

When it comes to elegance, the halo effect can significantly shape beliefs. The halo effect is a cognitive bias where individuals tend to assume that someone who is attractive in one way (e.g., physically appealing or elegantly dressed) is also attractive in other ways (e.g., intelligent or kind).

Research has shown that people often perceive elegant women as more competent and socially desirable. When someone is perceived as elegant through their appearance, demeanor, or behavior – this positive trait often leads others to assume that they have other desirable qualities, such as intelligence, kindness, or competence. For example, an elegantly dressed individual may be perceived as more sophisticated or knowledgeable, regardless of their actual abilities.

While the halo effect can lead to biased judgments, individuals who present themselves elegantly may be judged more favorably.

Due to the halo effect, individuals presenting as elegant may benefit from more attention and respect, which can create a self-reinforcing cycle. As they are treated with greater esteem, they may become more confident and continue to exhibit behaviors associated with elegance.

This self-reinforcing cycle, also known as a positive feedback loop, is a process in which a change in a system leads to further changes in the same direction, creating a cycle that amplifies the initial change.

Self-Reinforcing Cycle

Keep the concept of "self-reinforcing cycle" in mind as you embark on your journey toward a more elegant you.

In the field of elegance, this concept suggests that even a small change, to elevate one's level of elegance, triggers feedback and benefits that not only reinforce the initial change but leads to significant shifts in the same direction. This process continues, creating a cycle that can lead to rapid improvements (or declines), depending on the context.

For example. a self-reinforcing cycle can be seen in the context of a woman wearing a fragrance. When a woman chooses to wear a particular fragrance that she believes expresses her persona, a self-reinforcing cycle can emerge that reinforces her identity and enhances her experiences.

When wearing the fragrance, she receives compliments from others or notices a boost in her own confidence and mood. The fragrance may evoke positive feelings, reinforcing her choice to wear it. Because of the positive feedback and feelings associated with the fragrance, she is more likely to wear a fragrance regularly. Friends and acquaintances might start to think of her when they encounter that particular scent, further cementing its role in her identity.

This can lead to further compliments or social interactions that enhance her self-esteem and enjoyment. This can lead to a stronger association between wearing a fragrance and positive experiences.

Over time, the fragrance becomes a key part of her personal identity or self-expression. The cycle reinforces her belief in her persona, making her feel more authentic and confident in who she is.

Through this process, the fragrance not only serves as a personal signature but also plays a significant role in her emotional well-being and social interactions, enhancing her overall experience of self-expression and identity.

The self-reinforcing cycle applies to all things perceived as elegant, including fashion, lifestyle choices, behaviors, and even social interactions. Implementing any change toward a more elegant you will reinforce that initial change and lead to significant shifts in the same direction.

Cultural Standards and the Halo Effect

Different cultures have specific ideals of beauty and femininity, often associated with elegance. Studies have shown that individuals who adhere to these standards may be viewed as more attractive, leading to greater interest.

Cultural standards of beauty and sophistication can amplify the halo effect regarding elegance. Different societies may have varying definitions of what constitutes elegance, but in many cultures, traits associated with elegance – such as refinement, grace, and style – are highly valued and can lead to disproportionate positive perceptions.

Elegance is often linked to social status and refinements, which can add to a person's allure. Individuals who seem to embody sophistication may also be seen as more powerful or influential, which can also be attractive to many.

Confidence is a significant aspect of this allure. Elegant individuals often exude self-assurance, which is universally attractive. Their confidence signals self-worth and assurance, traits that many find appealing. The graceful movements of someone who is confident are visually captivating. The way an elegant person carries themselves – poised and composed – draws attention and admiration.

The combination of elegance and social poise can create a charismatic presence that draws people in. An elegant person often has a charismatic quality that can light up a room. This combination of confidence and charm can make social interactions feel more engaging and enjoyable.

Elegance is often associated with a breadth of knowledge and cultural interests. An appreciation for art, literature, music, or gourmet food can create stimulating conversations and connections with others who value similar qualities.

With elegance there is also a sense of mystery. An elegant woman may not reveal everything about herself right away, sparking curiosity and intrigue. People are often drawn to those who seem to have layers to uncover.

Emotional Influence and the Halo Effect

The perception of elegance can evoke positive emotions in others, such as admiration and aspiration. This emotional response can further enhance the halo effect, as individuals may project their feelings onto the elegant person, attributing them with extra charisma or charm.

Elegance often embraces subtlety rather than overt flamboyance. This understated quality can be more alluring, as it invites others to engage and discover nuances of the individual.

The display of social grace and etiquette makes those around an elegant person feel comfortable and valued. Their ability to navigate social situations with ease can enhance their desirability.

Elegance can be associated with positivity and grace in social interactions. People are often drawn to those who uplift and inspire them. An elegant woman who brings a sense of positivity and upliftment to social settings embodies an energy that contributes to an inviting atmosphere, making others want to be in their presence.

Emotional Intelligence

Emotional Intelligence, also referred to as emotional quotient, is the ability to recognize, understand, manage, and influence emotions – both your own and those of others. It involves a range of skills and competencies that are essential for personal well-being, effective communication, and relationship building. Emotional intelligence involves self-awareness – the ability to recognize and understand your own emotions, strengths, weaknesses, values, and motivations.

The qualities of emotional intelligence are the same qualities of individuals perceived as elegant. It is no surprise that elegant individuals display a high level of emotional intelligence, allowing them to connect with others on a deeper level. This ability to empathize and communicate effectively adds to their allure. Additionally, elegant individuals tend to be healthy mentally and have the ability to manage and regulate their emotions, particularly in stressful situations. They do not let their emotions dictate their actions. They are not melodramatic and are never referred to as "drama queens" or "divas". They think before acting and are able to pause before reacting to emotional triggers.

As individuals with a high level of emotional intelligence, elegant individuals also have a passion for what they do and a passion for a drive to achieve for the sake of personal fulfillment rather than external rewards.

In summary, studies related to emotional intelligence and the halo effect illustrate how the perception of elegance can shape the way individuals are viewed and treated in various contexts. Generally speaking, exhibiting elegance leads to positive perceptions.

"Elegance can be difficult to put into words, but it is unmistakable when seen or experienced." – Gina Judy

3

THE LANGUAGE OF ELEGANCE

Etiquette and social graces are the foundation of elegance. They silently guide our interactions and help us navigate the currents of social life. Like a beautiful ballroom, where the real performance is the dance of social grace, each step and conversation adds to the symphony of elegance.

Let's start with the table, the stage for our daily rituals of nourishment. Elegant dining is not about strict rules, but a mindful approach to eating. It's about savoring each bite, engaging in meaningful conversation, and expressing gratitude for the food before us. Forget rushed meals and instead envision a leisurely feast, where conversation flows like wine, laughter fills the room, and actions show respect for the food, company, and occasion. Take, for example, the use of utensils. Each has its own purpose and graceful movements. The fork gently guides food to our mouths, while the knife precisely cuts without force. Remember, it's not just about eating, but doing so with grace and refinement, a reflection of a cultivated demeanor.

In our daily interactions, we have endless opportunities to embody elegance. From simple gestures like a firm yet warm handshake to choosing our words carefully and listening actively, we can show respect, courtesy, and consideration towards others. Engaging in meaningful and respectful conversations rather than dominating opinions can also display our social grace. Our nonverbal communication, such as our posture, gestures, and eye contact, can convey our inner harmony and add a touch of refinement to our expressions. And politeness and respect should be the foundation of our interactions, as they are the invisible thread that weaves together the tapestry of elegance. By using phrases like "please," "thank you," and "excuse me," and extending kindness towards others, we can truly embody elegance in our everyday encounters.

Gratitude has immense power in nurturing elegance. Showing appreciation, no matter how small or big the act, reflects a refined understanding of the blessings in our lives. Gratitude is not just a formality, but a potent force that brings people together, promotes well-being, and fosters a positive and elegant perspective on life.

By embracing proper etiquette and social graces, you will discover a hidden doorway to an elegant world. It is a world where grace and refinement are not just superficial, but a way of life.

Exhibiting elegance speaks volumes. Just like a beautifully crafted piece of art, elegance is not solely about outward appearance, but the balance between inner and outer qualities, a symphony of poise and polish that resonates with the world around you.

Elegant Conversation

Elegant conversation involves communicating in a way that is more than just an opportunity to convey information. Elegant conversation is an art form that elevates both speaker and listener.

At the heart of elegant conversation is the ability to listen and truly engage with another person's thoughts and feelings. Active listening is not merely hearing the words but absorbing their meaning and recognizing the emotion. Active listening requires a conscious effort to focus on the speaker, to suspend judgment, and to seek understanding rather than just waiting for your turn to speak.

Imagine a room filled with people, each eager to share their thoughts, yet failing to truly listen. The conversation becomes a chaotic mixture of voices, each competing for attention ... the potential for genuine connection lost. But when active listening takes place, the conversation transforms into a shared journey of discovery.

Disagree Gracefully

The heart of respectful dialogue lies in the art of disagreeing gracefully, of navigating differing viewpoints with sensitivity and intelligence. Elegant communication certainly does not demand that everyone agree, but rather encourages the sharing of perspectives with open minds and respectful hearts. It is the ability to acknowledge the validity of another person's opinion, even if it diverges from your own, and to engage in a constructive exchange that enriches both parties.

Try to frame your thoughts in a way that invites other viewpoints and avoid interrupting, dismissing, or resorting to personal attacks.

Sometimes the most graceful or refined response to a disagreement is to remain silent rather than engage in conflict. A choice to not argue or to hold back one's opinion can show maturity, self-control, and a sense of dignity. It reflects the idea that sometimes stepping back and allowing space for reflection can be more powerful than trying to assert one's viewpoint.

Carefully Chosen Words

Elegant communication involves the ability to choose your words carefully and to speak with clarity and purpose. It is the art of finding the perfect phrase or turn of speech that captures the essence of your thoughts and provides meaning in the mind of the listener.

It is not about being the most eloquent or the most knowledgeable. It is about being genuinely present and engaging with others in a way that promotes understanding.

To illustrate the art of elegant communication, let us turn to the timeless words of fashion icon, Coco Chanel. Chanel weaves fabrics into stunning designs that speak to the essence of femininity and grace. Her words, like her creations, are carefully chosen and crafted with precision, evoking a sense of sophistication and refinement. As she famously said, "A girl should be two things: classy and fabulous." This simple yet powerful statement captures the essence of Chanel's elegant approach to fashion and life. She understood the power of words and used them to inspire women to embrace their femininity and to confidently express themselves through style. Chanel's words, like her iconic little black dress, have stood the test of time and continue to inspire generations. Chanel's words have a lasting impact, reflecting the timeless elegance of the woman behind them.

While there is no one-size-fits-all approach, an elegant communication style requires courteous language that shows respect for others.

Using the following polite words and phrases can enhance your communication and help create a positive atmosphere in conversation:

General Polite Expressions:

Please.

Thank you.

You're welcome.

Excuse me.

May I …?

Could I …?

Would you mind?

Polite Requests:

Would you be so kind as to …?

Could you please . . .?

I would appreciate it if you could . . . .?

If it is not too much trouble, could you . . .?

Responding to Opinions:

That's an interesting perspective.

I appreciate your input.

Thank you for sharing your thoughts.

I see your point.

Ending Conversations:

It was a pleasure speaking with you.

Thank you for your time.

I look forward to our next conversation.

Have a great day!

Expressing Gratitude:

I really appreciate your help.

Thank you for your understanding.

I'm grateful for your support.

Your help means a lot to me.

Making Suggestions:

Perhaps we could …

Would you consider …?

I think it might be beneficial to …

Apologizing:

I apologize for any inconvenience.

I'm sorry for the misunderstanding.

Please forgive me for …

I regret any confusion caused.

Offering Help:

How can I help you?

Is there anything I can do for you?

Please let me know if you need anything.

I'd be happy to help if I can.

Do you use these polite words and phrases in your day-to-day conversations? If not, you may consider including some of these words or phrases in your day-to-day conversations when appropriate.

Strive to maintain a positive and uplifting tone. This creates a more pleasant atmosphere during conversations and interactions.

While some informal language can be acceptable in casual settings, an elegant woman often opts for language that is more refined, especially in formal or professional environments.

Different cultures have varying norms around language and decorum. What may be considered inappropriate in one culture might be acceptable in another. To ensure you project a polite language style, avoid the use of coarse language and curse words.

Speak with confidence and composure. Avoid filler words and hesitations that may undermine your message.

Some signs that you may need to improve your communication style include:

- Do you often find that others misunderstand your message or intention? If so, it could suggest you need to work on clarification.
- Do others often react defensively or negatively to what you say? If so, it could suggest your tone or choice of words may be off-putting.

- Do discussions often escalate into arguments? If so, it could suggest the need to develop more effective conflict resolution and communication skills.
- Do you struggle to engage in conversations or find it hard to express your thoughts clearly? If so, you may need to work on improving your communication style.

Recognizing the need to improve your style of communication can be an important step toward personal and professional growth.

In a world filled with noise and distractions, the ability to engage in elegant conversation is a rare and valuable treasure. It is a gift that enriches both speaker and listener, fostering a sense of connection, understanding, and a shared appreciation for the power of human communication.

Non-verbal Communication

Imagine a world where every gesture, every movement, speaks volumes. Where a simple glance can convey volumes more than words ever could. This is the realm of non-verbal communication, and it is a cornerstone of elegance. In this world, elegance isn't just about the clothes we wear, but the way we carry ourselves, the presence we exude, and the messages we send without uttering a single word.

Think of a graceful swan gliding across a tranquil lake. Its every movement is fluid, purposeful, and captivating. It's a ballet of nature, a symphony of elegance in motion. Just as the swan's every gesture speaks of its inherent grace, our body language can speak volumes about our inner poise and confidence.

In recent conversation with a young twenty-something woman I was asked, "If there was one thing you would recommend to a woman seeking to be elegant, what would it be?" Without hesitation I answered, "Good posture . . . not only can it be accomplished immediately, but it costs nothing and can have the greatest impact on how others perceive you."

Your posture creates a visual impression. An upright stance, with shoulders back and head held high, exudes confidence and poise. The subtle tilt of the head, the relaxed position of the arms and legs, conveys your mood and attitude. Your posture is a silent language . . . it speaks volumes about your personality and state of mind. It's a visual representation of your emotions, from a relaxed and open stance when we are happy, to a slouched and closed-off position when we are feeling low. It's a reflection of our inner self, visible to the world without us speaking a single word.

Imagine walking into a room and feeling a surge of energy, an invisible wave of confidence washing over you. This is the power of posture, the subtle but powerful way we communicate our state of mind. A slumped posture, on the other hand, can project an air of insecurity, disinterest, or even apathy.

Then there are gestures, the language of the hands that can add emphasis to our words. A graceful gesture, whether it's a delicate hand movement to emphasize a point or a subtle wave of acknowledgment, can add a touch of elegance to any interaction. A hurried, flailing hand gesture, however, can detract from the refinement we aim to convey.

Eye contact can be extremely powerful. Direct eye contact is the key to conveying genuine interest and attention. It creates a connection, a shared moment, a feeling of being seen and heard. Avoiding eye contact, however, can convey disinterest, insecurity, or even dishonesty.

But elegance in non-verbal communication goes beyond mere physicality. It's also about presence, the aura of quiet confidence and attentiveness that radiates outward. It's the ability to be fully engaged in the moment, to listen with intent, to observe with curiosity, and to respond with thoughtful grace.

Think of a seasoned actor on stage, commanding the attention of the audience with a subtle shift in posture, a knowing glance, or a perfectly timed pause. This is an example of mastery in the use of silent language to captivate and draw others in.

As you embark on your journey to cultivate elegance, remember that non-verbal communication is more than just a skill; it's an art form, a language that requires practice, awareness, and a deep understanding of the subtle messages we send through our bodies and our presence. With time, dedication, and a mindful approach, you can master this silent language and truly embody the elegance that lies within.

Politeness and Respect

Politeness and respect are not merely social niceties; they are requirements of refined interactions. In a world often characterized by haste and a focus on self-interest, being polite and showing respect stand out as beacons of grace and civility.

Imagine a grand ballroom, its chandeliers casting a warm glow upon the gathered guests. As you enter, you are greeted by a symphony of murmurs and laughter, the clinking of glasses, and the soft strains of music. A palpable sense of anticipation and camaraderie is in the air. In this environment every interaction is an opportunity to show politeness and respect. In this situation, begin with the simple act of a warm smile and a sincere greeting. Address others, using proper and respectful language . . . acknowledge their presence with genuine warmth. Politeness dictates that you may help when needed, hold doors open for others, and show consideration for the comfort and well-being of those around you.

Respect, however, goes beyond manners. It is an acknowledgment of the inherent worth of every individual, regardless of their background, beliefs, or social status. It demands that we listen to others' perspectives, even if they differ from our own. It means engaging in dialogue with open-mindedness and empathy, seeking to understand rather than to judge. Respectful interactions are built on a foundation of trust, understanding, and mutual respect, where differences are not seen as obstacles but as opportunities for growth and learning.

The power of politeness and respect lies in their ability to transform ordinary interactions into moments of elegance. A simple "thank you" can shift the tone of a conversation, fostering a sense of appreciation and gratitude. A genuine compliment can brighten someone's day, creating a ripple effect of positivity. These small gestures, when woven together, create a tapestry of civility and warmth, reminding us of the inherent beauty of human connection.

In the realm of elegance, politeness and respect are not merely optional additions; they are the very essence of refined interaction. They are the silent language of grace, speaking volumes without uttering a word.

The Power of Gratitude

Gratitude is a simple yet profound act. When we express gratitude with elegance, we elevate our interactions to a higher plane, transforming ordinary moments into expressions of grace and respect.

The elegance of gratitude lies not just in its outward expression but in its underlying sincerity. When we cultivate a mindset of gratitude, we develop a heightened awareness of the blessings in our lives, appreciating the contributions of others and recognizing the interconnectedness that binds us all.

In terms of personal relationships, gratitude is a powerful catalyst for strengthening bonds and fostering deeper connections. A heartfelt thank-you note, a thoughtful gift, a simple gesture of care – these acts of gratitude speak volumes about the value we place on those closest to us. They remind others that they are appreciated, cherished, and an integral part of our lives.

Think of gratitude as a delicate flower, nurtured by the warmth of sincere appreciation. When we express gratitude with grace and sincerity, we are not only acknowledging the kindness of others but also cultivating a positive and generous spirit within ourselves. This reciprocal act of giving and receiving fosters a cycle of appreciation, enriching our own lives and the lives of those around us.

Let's consider some practical ways to incorporate the elegance of gratitude into our lives:

Mindful Appreciation

Cultivate a practice of mindful appreciation. Take a moment each day to reflect on the good things in your life, both big and small. Acknowledge the people who have made a positive impact, the experiences that have brought you joy, and the simple pleasures that often go unnoticed.

Expressing Gratitude Through Words

Make a conscious effort to express gratitude through words. Say "thank you" sincerely and often, both to those you know well and to strangers who extend kindness your way. Say "I really appreciate your help" or "I'm grateful for your support." Or express appreciation for someone's patience with the simple phrase, "Thank you for understanding" or "I appreciate your patience."

Take the time to write heartfelt notes of appreciation to those who have touched your life. These simple acts of verbal gratitude can make a profound difference.

Gestures of Appreciation

Beyond words, show gratitude through meaningful gestures. Spending time together, such as going out for coffee or a meal, can show that you value the person and appreciate their presence in your life.

After someone has helped you or done something significant, following up with a message or call to express your gratitude reinforces your appreciation.

A small gift, a handwritten note, an offer of help, a thoughtful act of service – these gestures speak volumes about your appreciation and create a ripple effect of positivity.

Tips and Gratuities

Tips and gratuities are gestures of appreciation, especially in the service industries. Leaving a tip is a direct way of acknowledging the hard work and effort that service staff put into providing a positive experience. It shows that you value the quality of service received, which can motivate service providers to continue delivering excellent service. Generosity in tipping can also contribute to a positive atmosphere in restaurants, hotels, and other service venues, benefiting both staff and patrons.

Failure to leave a tip could show a lack of social skills or suggest to others that you lack empathy for those who rely on tips. Both characteristics of an individual that lacks elegance and grace.

In many cultures, tipping is a standard practice, and it reflects social norms about gratitude and appreciation for service. This is true in the United States, France, Canada, and the United Kingdom.

In some cultures, tipping is not expected. In the countries of Italy, Spain, Sweden, Norway, Germany and Denmark, service charges are already included in the price.

In these countries, however, leaving small change or rounding up the bill is appreciated. And in a few countries, tipping is discouraged. In Japan, for instance, a monetary gratuity may be considered rude or could embarrass the staff.

Being aware of tipping customs in different regions can show respect for local practices and enhance interactions with service staff.

While a tip or gratuity serves as a tangible expression of gratitude, complementing and offering verbal thanks reinforces your appreciation.

I remember the day I stepped into my favorite nail salon for some much-needed pampering. After a long week of travel, my feet were begging for a pedicure, and my hands were in desperate need of a manicure. As always, the salon was bustling with customers, and the sound of chatter and laughter filled the air.

I took a seat, and my favorite pedicurists welcomed me with a warm smile. I couldn't help but feel a sense of calm wash over me as I settled into the plush massage chair. As the pedicurist worked his magic, we engaged in light conversation. He shared stories about his week and his plans for the weekend.

I could tell he was passionate about his job and took great pride in his work. After he finished, I couldn't help but admire the intricate details of my pedicure.

In addition to a monetary gratuity, I thanked him and praised his artistic and technical skills. In return he responded with genuine gratitude. He explained that in today's fast-paced world, people often forget to express appreciation, and it meant a lot to him. His words made me realize the importance of showing gratitude and acknowledging others for their hard work.

In the midst of our busy lives, we often forget to slow down and appreciate the little things. My visit to the nail salon not only left me with beautifully manicured nails, but also a valuable lesson in gratitude.

To show genuine grace and appreciation, don't forget to accompany monetary tips and gratuities with verbal appreciation. You will find that when expressing thanks, you become a key player in creating a culture of kindness and appreciation that leads to a pleasant environment for everyone.

Cultivating a Grateful Heart

Embrace a grateful heart as a way of life. Cultivating a grateful heart can have profound effects on both personal well-being and relationships with others.

Gratitude helps shift focus from negative thoughts to positive ones, reducing feelings of stress and anxiety. According to studies, practicing gratitude increases levels of happiness and life satisfaction, leading to a more positive outlook on life.

This positive outlook contributes significantly to an individual's elegance, both in demeanor and in how they are perceived by others. A positive outlook often fosters greater self-confidence. When you feel good about yourself and your abilities, you carry yourself with poise and grace, which are hallmarks of elegance.

Individuals with a positive attitude tend to be more gracious and courteous in their interactions. This kindness and consideration for others also contributes to a sense of refinement and elegance.

Positiveness can be contagious. When you exude a positive energy, you are more attractive to others, enhancing your overall elegance and appeal.

So, seek-out opportunities to express appreciation for the gifts, both large and small, that surround you. Look for the good in every situation, and practice finding joy in the simple things. By incorporating these practices into your daily life, you cultivate a spirit of gratitude that radiates outward and enriches the world around you.

The elegance of gratitude encourages a beautiful and more fulfilling life.

"Elegance . . . you know it when you see it."
– Gina Judy

4

THE ART OF SELF PRESENTATION

Confidence, that unshakeable belief in oneself, is the bedrock upon which true elegance rests. It is not merely about outward appearances; it is an inner strength that radiates outward, shaping our demeanor, influencing our choices, and defining how we present ourselves to the world. Imagine an exquisitely crafted piece of art, flawless in its form and composition, yet lacking the artist's touch, the undeniable energy that breathes life into it. This is the essence of elegance without confidence: a beautifully assembled facade without the soul to bring it to life.

Imagine, for instance, a woman standing in a room filled with people, dressed in an exquisite gown, yet her posture is slumped, her gaze hesitant. Her elegant attire is overshadowed by a lack of self-assurance, a hesitant whisper instead of a confident voice. Now envision the same woman, this time radiating with confidence. Her shoulders are straight, her eyes sparkle with engagement, her smile is genuine, and her every movement carries a sense of quiet power. The same elegant gown now becomes a canvas for her self-assured spirit, enhancing her presence, not defining it.

The connection between confidence and elegance is deeply intertwined with self-belief. When we believe in ourselves, our worth, and our abilities, it allows us to step into the world with a sense of purpose and grace. It's about recognizing our strengths, embracing our imperfections, and acknowledging that we are worthy of respect and admiration. This self-belief allows us to navigate social situations with ease, express our opinions with conviction, and engage in meaningful conversations without feeling the need to conform to external expectations.

Cultivating confidence, however, is not a one-time endeavor but a continuous journey of self-discovery and personal growth. It is about understanding our own values, setting realistic goals, and celebrating our achievements, big or small. It requires embracing our vulnerabilities, learning from our mistakes, and recognizing that growth often occurs outside our comfort zones.

Confidence

One powerful way to cultivate confidence is to focus on our strengths and celebrate our accomplishments. Instead of dwelling on our perceived weaknesses, we can choose to focus on what we do well, recognizing our unique talents and abilities. This can be as simple as acknowledging our accomplishments, whether it's mastering a new skill, completing a challenging project, or simply being a good friend. Each accomplishment contributes to a growing sense of self-belief and self-worth.

Another crucial aspect of building confidence is to embrace our imperfections. We are all human, with our unique flaws and quirks. Trying to achieve unattainable perfection only creates unnecessary pressure and undermines our ability to embrace our individuality. Embracing our imperfections allows us to be authentic, honest, and genuine, creating a sense of vulnerability that can be incredibly powerful in fostering connections and fostering a sense of self-acceptance.

Beyond self-belief, a positive self-image plays a crucial role in projecting elegance. It's about seeing ourselves through the lens of kindness and acceptance, recognizing our inherent value and potential. When we have a positive self-image, we are more likely to treat ourselves with respect, make choices that align with our values, and engage with the world with a sense of grace and self-assuredness.

Developing a positive self-image often requires challenging negative thoughts and beliefs. It's about recognizing self-defeating patterns, replacing them with empowering affirmations, and focusing on our positive attributes. It can also involve practicing self-care, engaging in activities that bring us joy, and surrounding ourselves with people who support and uplift us.

Confidence is not about arrogance or self-importance; it's about self-awareness and respect. It's about recognizing our own worth and potential, embracing our imperfections, and projecting a sense of ease and composure. It's about acknowledging our strengths, celebrating our achievements, and treating ourselves with the same kindness and respect that we would extend to others.

In the tapestry of elegance, confidence is the golden thread that binds together all the other elements: grace, poise, refinement, and style. It is the spark that ignites the inner flame, allowing us to radiate our unique beauty, both inward and outward. By cultivating a strong sense of self-belief and a positive self-image, we can unlock the true potential of elegance, not as a mere facade, but as a radiant expression of our authentic selves.

Poise and Graceful Movement

The art of graceful movement is often overlooked, yet it's an essential part of projecting an aura of elegance. It's not just about how you walk or stand; it's about the subtle cues your body language conveys, silently communicating your inner confidence and composure. Imagine a poised individual gliding across a room, each step a deliberate and purposeful action. They carry themselves with an effortless grace, their movements fluid and controlled. This is the essence of poise and grace, and it's something anyone can cultivate.

The foundation of graceful movement lies in posture, a silent language that speaks volumes about your self-assurance. A straight spine, shoulders back, and head held high creates a sense of presence and commands attention in a subtle yet powerful way. It's not about rigidity, but rather an alignment that exudes confidence and composure. Think of it as a delicate power pose, subtly conveying strength, and control. Imagine a queen walking through a ballroom, her back straight, her head held high, radiating an aura of authority and grace.

Gait, the way you walk, is another critical element in mastering the art of movement. A graceful gait is characterized by a smooth, effortless stride, with each step deliberate and controlled. Find a natural rhythm that complements your posture and allows your body to move with intention and purpose. Avoid hurried steps or shuffling feet; instead, imagine yourself walking on a stage, each step a calculated and confident move. Picture a model strutting down a runway, her every step exuding confidence and poise.

Gestures are like punctuation marks in the language of movement, adding emphasis and nuance to your expressions. Elegant gestures are deliberate, fluid, and purposeful. They can accentuate a point, add a touch of grace to your conversations, or simply convey a subtle sense of refinement. Observe how a conductor uses their hands to guide an orchestra, their gestures precise yet expressive.

Beyond the physical aspects of posture, gait, and gestures, graceful movement is also about embodying a sense of inner composure. It's about being present in the moment, aware of your surroundings, and moving with confidence and purpose. It's a state of mind that radiates outward, influencing how you navigate the world. Imagine a dancer gracefully navigating a complex routine, her movements flowing seamlessly, her mind calm and focused. This is the essence of graceful movement: a harmonious blend of physical control and inner composure.

Cultivating graceful movement isn't about achieving perfection but rather about finding a style that aligns with your personality and reflects your inner confidence. It's about recognizing the silent language of your body and using it to communicate elegance and poise. Here are a few practical tips to help you on your journey:

Pay Attention to Your Posture

Start by deciding whether you have good posture or not. Stand in front of a mirror and observe the alignment of your spine. Ideally, your head, shoulders, hips, and feet should be in a straight line. If you notice any excessive curves or misalignments in your spine, it may indicate poor posture.

Your spine has a natural curve that helps support your body. Check for the slight inward curve in your lower back, a slight outward curve in your upper back, and a slight inward curve in your neck.

Check the position of your shoulders. They should be relaxed and squared, not rounded, or hunched forward. Your pelvis should be in a neutral position, with your hips aligned over your ankles. Avoid excessive arching or tucking of the pelvis. Your knees and feet should be pointing forward, with your weight evenly distributed between both feet. Avoid locking your knees or standing with one foot turned out.

Good posture should feel comfortable and allow for ease of movement. If you experience pain, stiffness, or tension in your back, neck, or shoulders, it may be a sign of poor posture.

Make it a habit to regularly assess your posture, especially when sitting, standing, or walking. You can even use a mirror to check your alignment and adjust as needed.

Be mindful of your posture throughout the day. Sit up straight, avoid slouching, and keep your shoulders back. If you notice signs of poor posture, consider incorporating exercises, stretches, and ergonomic adjustments to encourage improvement. Correcting misalignments and imbalances will improve your posture over time.

A strong core provides support for your spine and helps maintain proper alignment. Incorporate exercises such as planks, bridges, and abdominal crunches to strengthen your core muscles.

Stretching can help alleviate tight muscles and improve flexibility, which can contribute to better posture. Focus on stretching your chest, shoulders, hips, and hamstrings to counteract the effects of prolonged sitting.

You may also consider seeking advice from a healthcare professional or posture specialist to obtain personalized guidance on improving your posture.

Practice Conscious Walking

Become aware of your gait. Pay attention to the length of your steps, the movement of your arms, and the rhythm of your walk. Imagine yourself walking with a sense of purpose, with each step deliberate and confident.

Select a straight line visual on an open floor space, this might be a series of aligned tiles, and practice conscious walking in a straight line placing one foot in front of the other. Take long, confident strides with your feet pointed forward. Place one foot in front of the other, crossing slightly at the ankles to create a smooth and fluid motion. Until you master smooth movements, consider wearing lower straight heels before graduating to taller heels.

Walking with a book on your head is a classic technique used to improve posture, balance, and grace. Here's how you can practice this age-old technique:

- Start by selecting a book with a flat surface and stable weight. A hardcover book or a stack of books can work well for this exercise. Try this book for this exercise. It's a perfect size for your first exercise in walking with a book on your head.

- Stand up straight with your shoulders back, head held high, and chin parallel to the ground. Engage your core muscles to support good posture.
- Place the book on the top of your head, balancing it carefully. Start with a smaller book or stack of books to practice the technique before advancing to larger or heavier books.
- Begin walking slowly and steadily, focusing on maintaining the book's balance on your head. Take small, controlled steps and keep your movement smooth and fluid.
- As you walk, pay attention to your body alignment and balance. Try to keep your head level and centered, avoiding excessive tilting, or swaying that may cause the book to fall.

Walking with a book on your head can help improve your posture by promoting an aligned spine, engaged core muscles, and proper body mechanics. Use this exercise to reinforce good posture habits and body awareness.

Once you feel comfortable walking with a book on your head, increase the difficulty by using a heavier book or adding obstacles to navigate. Place a book on your head while sitting at a table then practice standing and sitting. Or challenge yourself by stepping up and down a simple series of steps.

Walking with a book on your head is a fun and effective way to refine your posture, balance, and grace.

Taking Your Seat

Sitting with elegance involves poise and comfort. Sit up straight with your back aligned and your shoulders relaxed but not slumped. Keep your legs together. Depending on what's comfortable, cross your legs at the ankles or knees.

When crossing your legs at the knees, slightly angle your legs to the left if you are crossing your right leg over your left knee. Slightly angle your legs to the right if you are crossing your left leg over your right knee. Crossing your legs should be graceful and poised. Avoid swinging your leg back and forth.

When crossing your legs at the ankle or keeping your legs parallel, remember to keep your knees together.

If you are sitting on the floor tuck your legs to the side or sit with your legs together in front of you, crossing at the ankles.

Place your hands neatly in the center or to one side of your lap.

To create a flattering elegant sitting position, strive for a soft "S" shape by placing your hands neatly to the left, knees to the right, and ankles to the left. Of course, a subtle "S" can also be created with the opposite side – placing your hands neatly to the right, knees to the left, and ankles to the right. As long as you maintain good posture, a slight "S" seated position can be slenderizing and will photograph beautifully.

To illustrate, think of Kate Middleton, Duchess of Cambridge. Note her posture, demeanor, and elegance. Kate often sits with a straight back, exuding grace, and confidence. When seated, she may cross her legs at the ankles, a classic and refined sitting style that contributes to her elegant appearance. Her hands are usually placed neatly on her lap or resting gently on the armrests. This poised position reflects her calm demeanor and attentiveness, embodying the refined grace expected of a member of the royal family.

Practice these suggestions while viewing your sitting position and posture in a full-length mirror. With consistent practice, you will discover the most graceful sitting position for you.

Clapping and Waving

Whether it is waving or clapping your hands, make sure you are not moving your hands wildly or in front of your face. To clap your hands, keep your hands relaxed and your fingers slightly apart. This helps create a softer look. Keep your clap gentle. Avoid clapping too loud or forceful. When clapping keep your hands slightly to the left and at chest level. This keeps the movement graceful and refined.

When you wave, angle your wrist slightly so that your palm is facing outward. This adds an elegant flair to your wave. Move your hand in a gentle, flowing motion. Instead of a quick wave, try a slow, smooth motion from side to side. Smile warmly and make eye contact with the group or individual to create a connection.

Gracefulness is the key. Enjoy the moment and let your personality shine through.

Enter and Exit a Car with Grace

The key to entering a car gracefully requires NOT stepping into the space or you'll have to separate your knees.

Stand close to the car door. If you are wearing a skirt or dress, gather the fabric to prevent it from getting caught in the door.

As you sit, lower yourself gracefully by bending at your knees. Keep your knees together. Aim to keep your back straight as you transition to the seat. Once seated, bring your legs into the car keeping your knees together. If you are wearing a dress, you may want to adjust the fabric to ensure it is neatly arranged. If you are wearing a shorter skirt or dress, you can strategically use your hand with your handbag in front of you or on your lap as a shield from onlookers or cameras.

Once inside the car, adjust your posture to sit up straight, maintaining an elegant demeanor. Always secure your seatbelt with smooth graceful movements.

The key to exiting a car gracefully requires NOT stepping out of the space or you'll have to separate your knees. Move your legs out of the car at the same time, keeping your knees together. If you are wearing a skirt or dress, you can strategically place your hand with your handbag in front of you or on your lap as a shield from onlookers or cameras.

In instances where a driver or chivalrous gentleman opens your door, enter and exit the car in the same way. The driver or gentleman will serve as a shield from onlookers or cameras.

Embrace the Power of Gestures

Observe how people use gestures in conversation. Notice the subtle nuances of hand movements, facial expressions, and body language. Practice incorporating gestures that feel natural and expressive.

First and foremost, take good care of your hands. Make sure your hands are moisturized, always clean and well- manicured. Carry hand cream in your bag and have hand cream available in your office, and on your nightstand to maintain your hands.

To get comfortable with elegant hand gestures, practice by "warming up" your hands first. Stretch your arms in front of you, relax your wrist and make circles with your wrists. Put your hands together and create a wave. These types of exercises help relax your hands and make it easier to perform smooth and fluid movements that are essential for elegant gestures.

Learn the hand gestures that are in synch with the verbal message you are saying. If you gently move your hand upwards while you mention something about the growing number of individuals, your hand gesture goes with your message. If you talk without some hand gestures, it can be perceived as less than authentic.

When you are uncomfortable or unsure what to do with your hands, occupy them with something. Having a handbag or a champagne flute to hold is a perfect way to keep your hands occupied. When holding a wine glass or champagne flute, gently hold the stem rather than the bowl. Not only does this look more elegant, but it also keeps the bowl from warming and keeps the champagne chilled.

When holding a champagne flute or wine glass, hold the glass in your left hand so your right hand is free for a greeting. Use a napkin around the glass so your hands do not get wet. If you wish, transfer to the right hand to take a sip.

When you do not have a handbag or something to keep your hands occupied, you may use a gentle hand clasp or "hand dangle" as a feminine gesture. Lightly clasping your hands can be elegant resting on your lap or on the edge of a tabletop. A gentle hand dangle refers to a specific way to position the hands where one or both hands are relaxed and moving in a loose manner or slightly hanging from the wrist. In a feminine context, it can imply a more delicate or graceful demeanor.

Use gentle and fluid hand movements that flow naturally with your body language. Avoid abrupt or jerky motions and aim for smooth, graceful gestures. Keep your hands relaxed and avoid clenching your fists, holding them too stiffly, or placing them in your pockets. Allow your fingers to be subtly curled and maintain a soft open palm.

Use light touches or gestures to emphasize a point or convey emotion. For example, lightly touching your fingertips to your chest or chin can add a subtle elegance to your movements.

Use your hands to frame your face or express emotions. Lightly brushing your fingers along your jawline or gesturing near your eyes can add a touch of elegance to your gestures.

Be mindful where you place your hands during conversations or presentations. Avoid fidgeting or excessive hand movements and keep your hands comfortably positioned at your sides or in a relaxed gesture.

While pointing at a place or a thing may be appropriate to the situation, never point at an individual. Pointing at people is considered rude. Any hand gesture towards another individual should be completed with a full hand.

Lean slightly forward to show engagement and interest in conversations or presentations. Avoid slumping back in your chair or leaning too far forward. Find a balanced and comfortable position that exudes elegance.

Make smooth and deliberate movements when adjusting your position or transitioning from sitting to standing. Avoid sudden or jerky movements that can disrupt your elegant demeanor.

Again, take a cue from the graceful movements of Kate Middleton, who is known for her poise and elegance. She is subtle and mindful of her movements. She avoids distracting and excessive gestures.

Watch a video of Kate Middleton holding a clutch or accepting flowers from a fan. Try to practice gentle hand movements by practicing holding objects.

She will gently hold her clutch with one hand to the side or both hands in front of her body. When accepting flowers, she will extend her hand in a fluid motion that is barely noticeable. If she lowers her body to receive flowers from a child, she uses core muscles to maintain her posture. Strong core muscles act as an invisible corset. Notice her hands move gracefully with limited movement and her gaze is thoughtful and reassuring.

Using elegant gestures conveys poise, confidence, and sophistication in various social and professional settings. When using them it is essential to be intentional and deliberate with your movements and remember that less is more when it comes to body language and gestures.

Covering Your Mouth

There may be occasions when you must elegantly handle a tickle in your throat in public. On these occasions, you should move your left hand gracefully over your mouth. Do not use your right hand. Your right hand is the hand that you likely use to shake hands when you greet someone, and using your left hand to cover your mouth reduces the spread of germs.

Find Your Rhythm

Establishing a rhythm helps support balance and coordination. A consistent pace and stride length enables smoother movements, reducing the likelihood of stumbling or awkwardness.

A rhythmic walk also encourages proper posture. When you walk with a steady rhythm, you are more likely to keep your head up, shoulders back, chest open and spine straight, contributing to a more elegant appearance. Rhythm creates a sense of fluidity in your movements. Walking with a steady cadence allows your body to flow naturally, making your steps look more graceful and effortless.

Experiment with different types of movement. Try walking with a little more grace, stretching with more fluidity, and even dancing to find your unique rhythm. Walking with better balance, posture, and fluidity boosts your confidence and overall presence.

People often describe this type of fluid, controlled movement as "grace."

Mindfulness in Motion

Integrate mindfulness into your daily movements. As you walk, drive, or perform routine tasks, focus on your breath, your body, and the present moment. This simple practice can help you cultivate a sense of inner composure that radiates outwards.

Consistency and mindfulness are key when it comes to improving posture.

Be patient and persistent in practicing these techniques, and gradually incorporate them in your daily routine to see lasting improvements in your posture.

If you have specific postural issues or concerns, consider seeking guidance from a physical therapist, chiropractor, or posture specialist for personalized advice and support.

Observe the Experts

Watch ballet dancers, actors, beauty pageant finalists, and other individuals known for their graceful movement. Pay attention to their posture, gait, and gestures. Observe how they move with intention and purpose.

Consider taking a class to learn professional walking techniques and tips from experienced instructors. Remember, an elegant walk is not just about physical technique but also about projecting confidence and poise. With patience, practice, and self-assurance, you can master a beautiful walk and make a lasting impression.

Practice Makes Perfect

Like any skill, mastering graceful movement takes practice. Make it a point to consciously work on your posture, gait, and gestures throughout the day. The more you practice, the more natural and effortless these movements will become.

Remember, graceful movement is more than just a physical skill; it's a reflection of your inner confidence and composure. It's about moving through the world with a sense of purpose and elegance. As you cultivate this aspect of self-presentation, you'll not only enhance your physical presence but also unlock a new level of confidence and poise. You'll radiate an aura of elegance, leaving a lasting impression on those around you.

The Elegant Smile

The elegant smile is a genuine smile. A genuine smile is a powerful tool in the arsenal of elegance. It's a universal language, understood across cultures and boundaries, which speaks volumes about our inner state and our approach to the world. A smile, when genuine, radiates warmth, approachability, and a sense of openness that instantly draws people in, fostering connections and creating a positive impression.

Imagine walking down a busy street, surrounded by the cacophony of city life. You catch the eye of a stranger, and a smile breaks across their face. In that fleeting moment, a connection is made. The smile, even if brief, offers a glimmer of human connection, transforming a potential encounter into a shared experience. It's a silent gesture of kindness, a subtle affirmation of shared humanity.

In the realm of social interactions, a smile can be a powerful icebreaker. It can ease tension, soften the edges of awkwardness, and create a more welcoming and comfortable atmosphere.

Think of a networking event, where you're surrounded by unfamiliar faces. A genuine smile, offered readily and sincerely, can make a significant difference in how you are perceived. It signals to others that you are approachable, open to conversation, and willing to connect. This openness, in turn, can lead to new friendships, valuable connections, and expanded social circles.

Beyond its social implications, a smile also has a profound impact on our own well-being. Studies have shown that the simple act of smiling can trigger the release of endorphins, chemicals in the brain that produce feelings of happiness and well-being. Smiling, even when we don't feel happy, can actually elevate our mood, helping to reduce stress and anxiety. In essence, a smile is a powerful tool for self-care, a simple yet effective way to boost our own happiness and create a more positive inner state.

The key to the power of a smile lies in its genuineness. A forced smile, strained and insincere, can actually have the opposite effect. It can come across as disingenuous and even unsettling. A genuine smile, however, emanates from within, reflecting a genuine warmth and positive intention. It's a smile that reaches the eyes, crinkles the corners of the mouth, and illuminates the face with a radiant glow.

Cultivating a genuine smile is an essential part of projecting elegance. It's a simple yet powerful gesture that speaks volumes about our inner state and our approach to the world. A genuine smile is a beacon of warmth, approachability, and kindness, making us more approachable, enhancing our social connections, and creating a positive impact on our own well-being. So, the next time you find yourself interacting with others, remember the power of a smile. Let it be your signature, a testament to your inner grace and a reflection of the elegance you carry within.

Grooming and Hygiene

Grooming and hygiene are not merely superficial concerns; they are integral to projecting an air of elegance. They reflect a respect for oneself and for those around you. Imagine an expertly tailored suit, impeccably crafted, yet marred by unkept hair or a visible lack of personal hygiene. The impact of such a discrepancy is undeniable, the carefully constructed facade of elegance crumbles under the weight of neglect.

A polished appearance begins with healthy, well-cared-for skin. Taking care of your skin is an investment in your overall well-being and appearance. This often involves proper skincare and, when applicable, subtle makeup that enhances features. A consistent skincare routine, tailored to your skin type, is essential. This may include gentle cleansing, toning, moisturizing, and exfoliating. Sun protection is paramount, as harmful UV rays can cause premature aging and damage.

Even though everyone's skin is different, the general guidelines for skin care include:

Morning: Cleanser
            Vitamin C Serum
            Moisturizer
            SPF Sunscreen

Evening:	Double Cleansing
	Toner
	A Targeted Serum
	Moisturizer
Other:	Exfoliation 1-3 Times Per Week
	Weekly Mask
	Retinoids 2-3 Times Per Week
	Facial Oils

Hair care is equally important. Hair should be clean, styled, and neat. Whether you prefer a sleek updo or a tousled mane, a well-groomed hairstyle adds a touch of sophistication to your look. Regular trims, proper conditioning, and using hair products that enhance your natural texture are crucial for maintaining healthy and vibrant hair.

Consider consulting a stylist for professional advice on the best hair care routine and style to suit your face shape and personal style. Once you identify the best routine for your hair, make your routine a habit so you are always taking care of your hair, not just when it is damaged.

Additionally consult your doctor about the best vitamins and minerals to support your hair needs. It is common for medical professionals to recommend Biotin, Protein, Multivitamins, Collagen, and Keratin.

While we often focus on the external aspects of grooming, the essence of elegance lies in a healthy lifestyle that promotes both inner and outer radiance. A balanced diet, sufficient hydration, and regular exercise not only improve physical well-being but also radiate outward in the form of a healthy glow and energetic demeanor.

Proper attire complements good grooming, signifying both a sense of respect for the occasion and a commitment to presenting oneself in a refined manner. Choose garments that fit well, flatter your figure, and are appropriate for the context. A well-chosen outfit speaks volumes about your attention to detail and your understanding of the unspoken language of elegance.

Beyond the immediate physical aspects, grooming and hygiene encompass a deeper layer of self-care. It's about taking pride in your appearance and showing a commitment to personal well-being. Elegance is about presenting your best self, both inside and out. By attending to the details of grooming and hygiene, you cultivate a sense of self-respect and create a foundation for a more refined and confident presence.

Think of it as a quiet confidence that resonates beyond the surface. It's a subtle aura of polish and refinement that finely communicates your attention to detail and your commitment to presenting yourself in the best possible light. This, in turn, creates a positive impression and enhances the impact of your words and actions.

Consider the elegance of a meticulously crafted piece of art. Every brushstroke, every curve, every subtle shade contributes to the overall harmony and beauty of the work. In the same way, the elements of grooming and hygiene – skincare, hair care, attire, and a healthy lifestyle – work together to create a cohesive and elegant picture of your overall presence.

By embracing the principles of grooming and hygiene, you not only elevate your appearance but also cultivate a deeper sense of self-awareness and personal pride. This, in turn, empowers you to move through the world with confidence and grace, radiating an undeniable aura of refinement. Remember, true elegance is not simply about external appearances; it's about the embodiment of a refined spirit and a commitment to personal excellence.

Are Tattoos Elegant?

The perception of tattoos has evolved significantly over the years and people now view them as a form of self-expression, artistry, and personal storytelling. And while societal views on tattoos have shifted, and they are increasingly accepted, an elegant lady may choose more subtle, delicate tattoos that can be easily hidden or shown, depending on her outfit and the occasion.

Elegance is often about confidence and self-assuredness. A woman who embraces her tattoos as part of her identity can definitely exude confidence. On the other hand, a highly visible tattoo that reduces a woman's level of confidence or fails to reflect the image a woman wishes to portray is a tattoo that may have outlived its allure. In these situations, the elegant woman may consider covering or removing a tattoo.

Removing tattoos permanently can be a complex and often costly process. The most common and effective method for tattoo removal is through the use of a laser. When your medical professional recommends this process, a laser is used to break down the ink particles in the skin which allows the body to gradually absorb them. Depending on the size, color, and depth of the tattoo, multiple sessions may be required. Other options for removal include dermabrasion, chemical peels, or surgical excision. The options for these removal processes vary and each present their own set of risks. Consultation with a qualified medical professional is crucial to discuss which option is the best fit for you.

I had always viewed my tattoo as a form of self-expression, but over time, my perspective on elegance evolved, and the tattoo no longer aligned with my vision. Seeking a change, I consulted a renowned plastic surgeon who suggested laser removal with a specialist as the ideal solution. I was apprehensive about the procedure, but my medical professional assured me that a medical-grade lidocaine solution would effectively numb the treatment area, minimizing discomfort. On the day of the procedure, I felt a mix of anticipation and nervousness. The cool sensation of the lidocaine solution being applied to my skin brought a sense of relief, knowing that the laser treatment would be more bearable. As the laser began to remove the tattoo, I felt a strange sensation, almost like a rubber band snapping against my skin, but the lidocaine solution did its job, and the discomfort was manageable. The laser removal process was a unique experience, and I felt a sense of transformation with each passing moment. Though the procedure was not without its challenges, the result was a step closer to my new definition of elegance. As the treatment concluded, I felt a sense of satisfaction, knowing that I had taken a bold step towards embracing a new version of myself.

Elegance is more about how you carry yourself, the choices you make, and the confidence with which you present those choices. Tattoos can be a part of that narrative. But, when a tattoo ceases to represent you, removal is an option to explore with your medical professional.

Etiquette and Manners

An elegant woman, with a graceful presence, understands that etiquette and manners are essential in navigating social situations with poise and respect. She knows that proper etiquette is about more than just following a set of rules; it is a way to show consideration for others and create a harmonious atmosphere.

An elegant woman knows that her drink glass is to her right and her bread plate is to her left during dinner. She also knows that proper dining etiquette dictates that she should not reach over or around other guests to get to her food. This shows her consideration for others and her ability to navigate formal dining situations with grace.

She is also aware of the importance of keeping her napkin on her lap throughout the meal. This small gesture not only shows her good manners, but also her level of comfort with formal dining etiquette. It is a subtle yet powerful indication of her upbringing and social status.

She chews with her mouth closed and finishes chewing before opening her mouth, this includes laughing and talking. She politely covers her mouth with her hand if she must speak or laugh.

Additionally, she refrains from placing her elbows on the table, showing her understanding of proper table manners. This simple act shows her attentiveness and respect for the dining experience.

An elegant woman will use her napkin to wipe her fingers. She will never lick her fingers. She will place the napkin on her lap and will use it to dab the corners of her mouth.

When finishing your meal, the proper etiquette for napkin placement involves placing your napkin neatly to the left of your place. This is often seen as a polite way to indicate to the server that you have completed your meal and are ready for the table to be cleared.

The elegant woman's understanding of etiquette and manners extends beyond the dinner table. She is mindful of her surroundings and adapts her behavior to suit the situation. When entering a room, she does so with purpose and a gentle air of confidence. Her posture is upright, exuding an innate sense of grace and poise. She greets others with a warm smile and a gentle tone, creating an instant connection and putting people at ease. This woman understands the power of a simple greeting and a sincere inquiry about one's day. Her manners are not just reserved for formal settings, but she also embodies them in her daily life.

When engaging in conversation, she listens attentively, maintaining eye contact and nodding encouragingly, demonstrating her engagement and respect for the speaker. Her responses are thoughtful and considerate, avoiding interruptions or speaking over others.

This graceful woman is mindful of her tone, ensuring it remains pleasant and friendly, especially when disagreeing or facing differing opinions. In her interactions, she values kindness and empathy. She offers genuine compliments and expresses gratitude freely, creating a positive atmosphere wherever she goes.

Whether it's offering a sincere apology when necessary or simply being mindful of her volume in public spaces, she respects the comfort and personal space of those around her.

She is mindful of her body language, ensuring it aligns with her respectful nature. This elegant woman understands that true elegance is reflected in how one treats others, regardless of the circumstance.

When it comes to hosting, this graceful woman is the epitome of hospitality. She ensures her guests feel welcomed and valued, tending to their needs with warmth and attention to detail. From the moment they arrive, she creates a comfortable and engaging atmosphere. Her home is an extension of her elegant persona, with thoughtful touches and a serene ambiance. She offers refreshments with a smile, presenting them with the same care and attention as a five-star establishment.

This elegant woman understands that etiquette and manners are not just about following rules but about fostering meaningful connections and creating a pleasant environment for all.

Etiquette Guidelines

Proper etiquette is essential for making a favorable impression and ensuring a pleasant experience for yourself and others.

When receiving invitations, always RSVP right away.

Dressing appropriately for the occasion and setting shows respect for your hosts and fellow guests or diners.

Always arrive on time for your reservation or gathering. Being late can disrupt the flow of the meal.

Allow the host to guide you to your seat. If you are at a formal event, follow their lead.

Try to learn the names of others and use their names when you see them. While there are tricks to remembering names, my best advice is to simply focus on the person if you want to remember their name. If the conversation lends itself to repeating the individual's name, this can help – but do not force this technique.

Exhibit good posture when mingling and sit up straight when seated. Avoid slouching or leaning on tables or furniture.

Use polite terminology throughout the day. "Please," "thank you," and "excuse me" are some examples of generally polite things to say. Sometimes sending a handwritten thank you note or gift to express appreciation can show heartfelt gratitude.

Observe your surroundings and be sensitive to situations that call for kindness. For instance, let someone go in front of you in line if they have only a few items and you are buying several.

Avoid spreading germs. For instance, cover your nose and mouth when you cough or sneeze. Ideally use a tissue or handkerchief and cleanse your hands immediately after the cough or sneeze.

Do not assume everyone wants to have their names or photographs on social media. Do not post a photo or make a comment using someone else's name without their consent.

Keep your phone in silent mode and put it away during meals and events to show respect for the event and other guests present.

Pay attention to your surroundings and be courteous to guests and any support or wait staff.

Participate in polite conversation and make sure to include everyone at the table or in your surroundings. Avoid controversial or overly personal topics.

Handbag and Clutch Etiquette

Handbag etiquette involves understanding the appropriate ways to carry, place, and care for your handbag.

Select a handbag size that is appropriate for your frame and the occasion. Extra-large handbags can overwhelm women with smaller frames and micro handbags may appear juvenile on taller silhouettes. Smaller bags are often more suitable for formal events and larger bags can be used for casual outings.

Whether you are carrying a clutch or a top handle bag, always carry on the left side. This allows you to offer your right hand to greet someone without having to move your bag to the other hand.

A top-handle handbag should be carried in the crook of your left arm, your left hand, or your left shoulder. When in the crook of your left arm at the elbow, your forearm should extend upward with your left palm facing up and your fingers gently clasped.

A clutch should always be held by the hands and never under the pit of your arm.

When dining never place your handbag on top of the table. Never sling the long handle or strap of a bag over your chair. Instead place your bag on a vacant chair or stool. To prevent your bag from getting soiled, avoid placing your handbag on the floor. In addition to preventing dirt and bacteria from collecting on your bag, placing a handbag on the floor is considered bad luck in many cultures.

When a vacant chair or stool is not available and you would like to avoid placing your bag on the floor, you may consider using a purse hook if available.

Given the smaller size of a clutch, it may rest on your lap underneath your napkin.

Ensure your handbags and clutches are clean and in good condition. Store them properly when not in use, ideally in a dustbag or a cool, dry place away from sunlight and humidity. To maintain their shape, consider using bag shapers or inserts specifically designed to maintain the shape of the bag. Some bags come with foam or plastic shapers that fit inside to help retain their structure. If your bag doesn't have one, you can purchase a generic insert that fits well. You may also simply stuff with tissue, bubble wrap, or a soft cloth. This is especially useful for structured bags that may lose their form over time.

To prevent stretching the straps, avoid hanging your bag from hooks or doorknobs and be mindful of the items you carry. Excessive weight can stretch the materials and alter the bag's shape. Regularly check for unnecessary items and declutter your bag often.

Conversation Etiquette

Good conversation etiquette is essential for fostering positive interactions and maintaining a respectful atmosphere.

Sometimes when you see someone you are not certain if you have met them before or you think there is a possibility that you have met them online or on social media. In these situations, it can be awkward to say, "I am not sure if I have met you before." Instead, simply say, "It's nice to see you." This is something that works whether you have met the individual or not.

Remember to tailor your topics to suit the interests and comfort levels of those you are conversing with. Appropriate conversation topics include hobbies, travels, books, movies, or music that you and your conversation partner enjoy.

Feel free to share insights on non-controversial news items or local happenings as long as they do not delve into sensitive subjects. Sharing experiences about favorite restaurants, recipes, or cuisines can be delightful topics, especially if you are in a dining setting.

Talking about professional experiences, challenges, and aspirations can foster connection, but it's best to avoid excessive complaining or negativity.

Discussing shared experiences, events, and mutual friends can create a sense of camaraderie.

Light-hearted discussions about family members or pets can also be warm and inviting.

Inappropriate conversations include any discussions about political beliefs. Political topics can be divisive and lead to intense arguments so it's best to avoid this topic. Conversations about religious or spiritual beliefs and sharing overly personal stories or intimate experiences should also be avoided as they can be very personal and make others feel awkward or uncomfortable.

Asking about someone's income, debts, or financial struggles can also be intrusive and inappropriate.

Controversial issues like abortion, gun control, or other polarizing social issues can lead to tension and should be avoided in casual settings.

Avoid discussing private health matters or medical conditions as they can make others uncomfortable, especially in conversation.

Speaking negatively about others, spreading rumors, or engaging in gossip can reflect poorly on you and create an untrustworthy atmosphere.

When the conversation is appropriate, show genuine interest in what others are saying and respond appropriately. Maintain open and friendly body language and avoid crossing your arms or appearing disinterested.

Give your attention to the person speaking and avoid distractions such as your phone or other conversations. Nod, maintain eye contact, and provide verbal affirmations (like "I see" or "That's interesting") to show you are listening.

Avoid interrupting when others are speaking. Let the other person finish their thoughts before responding. If you need to interject, do so politely.

Use questions that require more than a yes or no answer, prompting deeper conversation. For example, a question like "What do you enjoy most about your work?" encourages open dialogue.

To show interest, use favorable body language. Sitting or standing up straight conveys interest and confidence. While it is appropriate to use hand movements to emphasize your points and make the conversation more engaging, ensure those gestures are gentle and fluid in movement.

Ensure your voice conveys warmth and interest. Avoid sounding monotone, overly aggressive, or sarcastic. Sarcasm can be misunderstood and is not perceived as elegant.

Never use profanity.

Finally, be gracious and express gratitude when the situation warrants. When meeting someone new, for example, let them know it was nice to meet them.

Dress Codes

A dress code is an established set of rules that outlines what is considered proper attire in a particular setting. These codes vary depending on the context, whether it be for work, school, or a formal event. In a professional setting, dress codes are typically stricter and require employees to dress in a professional and conservative manner. This is to maintain a level of professionalism and project a certain image to clients or customers. On the other hand, dress codes in educational institutions tend to be more relaxed, but still have guidelines to ensure proper and respectful attire.

Dress codes in educational settings often prohibit clothing that is revealing or that promotes inappropriate messages. Dress codes in schools also aim to create a level playing field among students and avoid unnecessary distractions. In formal events, dress codes are often specified on the invitation and can range from casual to black tie.

These codes are put in place to create a specific atmosphere and ensure that everyone is dressed appropriately for the occasion. They also help guests know what to expect and how to dress accordingly.

Casual

A "casual" dress code typically refers to a relaxed and informal style of clothing that prioritizes comfort and personal expression while still being appropriate for various settings. For the elegant woman, a "casual" dress code may suggest a black cashmere turtleneck worn with white tailored denim jeans and black leather flats or white sneakers. With a casual dress code, accessories can allow for personal expressions without being overly formal. A smaller black leather Chanel cross body or Prada tote are options for a casual outfit.

Business Casual

A "business casual" dress code strikes a balance between formal business attire and casual wear. It allows for a more relaxed and comfortable style while still maintaining a professional appearance suitable for the workplace or business meetings. An elegant woman may consider a navy sheath or wrap dress with closed-toe mid-heel pumps and bold gold-tone jewelry for a business casual look. The key with "business casual" is to strive for a polished yet comfortable style that is appropriate for professional settings.

Professional

A "professional" dress code typically refers to a formal style of attire that is appropriate for traditional business environments, such as corporate offices, formal meetings, and professional events. A professional woman may select a camel tone tailored suit or structured dress with closed-toe pumps and understated jewelry. Accessorize with a structure top handle bag and a complimenting silk scarf.

The "professional" dress code emphasizes a polished and sophisticated appearance, reflecting professionalism and respect for the workplace.

Cocktail Attire

A "cocktail attire" dress code is sometimes referred to as a semi-formal dress code. This type of dress code is associated with social events, parties, and evening gatherings. The intent of this dress code is to strike a balance between formal and casual, allowing individuals to dress stylishly and elegantly while still being comfortable. An elegant woman may select a fitted cocktail dress that hits slightly above her knee and a pair of delicate patent high heel pumps with a matching patent clutch. A pair of modern, statement earrings or a slick ponytail with diamond stud earrings are perfect compliments for the "cocktail attire" silhouette.

"Festive" cocktail attire suggests clothing that is stylish and appropriate for holiday parties or celebrations. When the invitation details include Festive Cocktail Attire, feel free to wear festive colors, metallics, sequins, or crystal embellishments. Even though festive attire can feel fun and flirty, avoid all things inelegant. Holiday ornament style earrings, for example, may feel spirited but they lack the sophistication the host intends for the event.

The formality of the Cocktail Attire dress code can depend on the nature of the event and the specific invitation. It is always a good idea to consider the host's style and the event in coordinating the ideal outfit for these situations.

Black Tie

The "black tie" dress code is sometimes referred to as a dress code calling for formal attire. This dress code is typically associated with upscale events such as galas, formal weddings, charity balls, and other elegant evening functions. It emphasizes sophistication, elegance, and a polished appearance. An elegant woman will want to strive for an overall look of sophistication and refinement. A long or below the knee length dress with a rhinestone embellishment worn with stylish high heeled evening pumps and matching rhinestone clutch is a consideration. Hair should be styled in an elegant fashion, which can include updos, soft waves, or sleek straight looks. Makeup should be polished and can be more dramatic than an everyday look.

Always pay attention to the specifics provided on the invitation, as some events may have additional guidelines or variations in what is acceptable for "black tie" attire.

White Tie

"White tie" attire has its roots in 19th-century formal wear and is considered traditional and ceremonial. It is the most formal dress code and is typically reserved for the most prestigious events, such as state dinners, formal balls, and certain high-profile weddings. It is the pinnacle of elegance and sophistication, requiring meticulous attention to detail and adherence to traditional standards.

An elegant woman will select a full-length evening gown made of luxurious fabric and may include intricate details such as lace or beading. Elegant accessories such as statement jewelry or evening gloves can be considered. Frequently high heeled evening shoes and clutch will match or compliment the evening gown.

At the inaugural ball on January 20, 1961, Jackie Kennedy, the wife of President John F. Kennedy, wore a stunning and iconic gown designed by Oleg Cassini. The evening dress was a floor-length, soft pink silk gown that featured a boat neck, fitted bodice and long sleeves. Jackie accessorized the gown with matching pink silk scarf, elegant gloves, and a strand of pearls with diamond earrings. Her hair was styled in a chic updo, and her makeup was understated.

The gown was notable for its simplicity and timeless grace and sophistication. Jackie's appearance at the ball was widely praised and perfectly illustrates "white tie" elegance. This is a notable vision to keep in mind when considering what is appropriate for attending a "white tie" event.

Overall, dress codes serve a purpose in different settings and help maintain a certain standard of dress.

Table Etiquette

There are two dining styles, Continental and American.

Continental dining style, also known as European style or German style, is a way of eating that involves holding the fork in the left hand and the knife in the right hand. The fork tines should face down.

American style, or Zigzag, occurs when you cut the food with your right hand and then switch hands to eat with your right hand.

A good general rule is to use utensils from the outside in. For multiple courses, start with the outermost utensils and work your way in as each course is served. If dessert is served, you will find dessert utensils positioned at the top of your plate.

Take small bites and chew with your mouth closed. Do not talk when eating and keep pace with your fellow diners to maintain a comfortable dining rhythm.

If someone asks for something across the table, pass it directly to them rather than reaching over others.

When you take a sip of your beverage, do not make eye contact. Instead, look down into your glass.

When you are done eating, place your utensils parallel on your plate (handles facing right) to signal that you have finished.

Regardless of whether you were hosted at a restaurant, someone's home, or at an event, express gratitude to your host. If dining at someone's home, offer to help clear the table or wash dishes as a gesture of appreciation.

Proper Use of a Napkin

By using her napkin thoughtfully, an elegant woman exemplifies grace and attention to etiquette, embodying poise during meals. Using proper dining etiquette enhances her own dining experience and the atmosphere around her. Upon being seated, she gently unfolds her napkin and places it on her lap.

If the napkin is large, she folds it in half with the fold facing her waist and the edges facing her knees. With the edges close, it is easy to pull up the corner edges of the napkin during the meal to gently blot with the inside then place back down. This leaves the outer part of the napkin clean and tidy.

Some ladies prefer placing the napkin with the fold facing the knees and the edges facing the waist. This makes accessing the napkin's corner edges a bit easier. Either is an elegant visual that ensures proper use of the inside of a napkin corner to blot the mouth gently, and then place the napkin back on your lap in a way that conceals any soiled areas.

If the napkin is small, she leaves it unfolded on her lap. When using, she gently picks up the napkin and uses the underside to dab the mouth area then repositions it on her lap.

If the napkin is folded into a triangle, she unfolds it under the table and refolds it into a rectangle to better cover her lap in case of spills.

If a restaurant wait-staff places the napkin on her lap, she permits assistance and discretely arranges the napkin if necessary.

If dining at a formal event, she waits for the host or hostess to unfold their napkin before unfolding and placing her own napkin.

Throughout the meal, she uses her napkin discreetly to dab her mouth as needed, demonstrating neatness and consideration for her appearance.

If she accidentally spills something, she remains composed, using the napkin to clean up the area subtly without drawing attention to the mishap.

When taking a break from eating, she places her napkin neatly on her lap signaling that she is not finished yet.

Once the meal is over, she places the napkin loosely to the left of her plate, indicating she has finished, without folding it or making it overly neat, as this is typically not expected in formal dining.

Squeezing A Lemon

An elegant lady squeezes a lemon during a meal with grace and consideration for etiquette.

If the lemon is served as wedges, she picks up a wedge with her fingers, ensuring her hands remain clean and composed.

With one hand she holds the lemon section over her glass or dish. She shields other diners from squirts by holding a spoon or cupping her other hand in front of the lemon as she squeezes.

To gently squeeze the lemon, she uses her thumb and forefinger to apply pressure without excessive force. This allows her to control the amount of juice that is released.

If she encounters seeds, she discreetly avoids them or removes them with a fork, maintaining her composure.

Some restaurants fit lemons with a cheesecloth covering to prevent these problems.

After squeezing the lemon, she may dab her fingers with her napkin if any juice has splattered, ensuring her hands remain clean and tidy.

Throughout the process, she maintains a pleasant demeanor and engages in conversation, showing that she is at ease and confident, regardless of the task at hand.

By following these guidelines, an elegant woman demonstrates not only her knowledge of dining etiquette but also her ability to handle small tasks with grace and poise.

These guidelines are merely a sample of proper etiquette and good manners. Proper etiquette and good manners are simply behaviors that show kindness.

When you are in doubt about what actions may be considered proper etiquette or good manners, reflect on the type of behavior or action that one could perform to show kindness to others. This type of consideration requires mindful presence.

Mindful Presence

The concept of mindful presence, a cornerstone of elegance, goes beyond simply being physically present in a space. It's about cultivating a focused awareness of your surroundings, your interactions, and the subtle cues that shape the social landscape.

Imagine yourself walking into a room. Instead of being lost in your thoughts or consumed by your phone, you actively observe the space, noticing the decor, the energy of the people in attendance, and the unspoken rules that govern the atmosphere. This attentive presence allows you to navigate social situations with grace and sensitivity, responding to subtle cues with poise and discretion.

Mindful presence is about attuning your senses. It's about listening attentively to conversations, observing body language, and interpreting the nuances of social interactions. It's about being genuinely present, engaging with the world around you, and demonstrating a genuine interest in others.

Imagine attending a formal event, a gala or a wedding. Instead of simply standing in a corner, you actively engage with the conversation, responding thoughtfully to what others say, and asking insightful questions. You notice the subtle gestures of the guests, the way they carry themselves, and the unspoken language of their interactions. This mindful presence allows you to navigate the social landscape with ease, contributing to the atmosphere of the event with grace and sensitivity.

This attentiveness extends beyond social gatherings. In everyday life, mindful presence helps you navigate the intricacies of human interaction. It allows you to recognize the unspoken needs of others, respond to their emotions with empathy, and demonstrate a genuine concern for their well-being. It's about being present in conversations, offering a listening ear, and recognizing the importance of thoughtful responses. It's about being present in your interactions, observing the cues that guide effective communication. This mindful presence fosters a sense of connection, deepening your relationships and enriching your experiences.

Mindful presence is not just about observing others; it's also about being aware of yourself. It's about recognizing your own emotions, managing your reactions, and responding to situations with composure and grace. It's about being present in your body, acknowledging your physical sensations, and projecting an aura of calm and confidence. Imagine a stressful situation, perhaps a demanding work meeting or a challenging personal interaction. Instead of reacting impulsively, you take a moment to breathe, center yourself, and approach the situation with composure. You listen actively, respond with respect, and navigate the challenges with a sense of inner peace. This mindful presence allows you to maintain your composure, even in difficult situations, and to project an air of tranquility that inspires confidence in those around you.

Cultivating mindful presence is a continuous journey, a practice that requires dedication and effort. It's about training your mind to be fully present, to engage with the world around you with intention and awareness. Here are a few techniques that can help you cultivate mindful presence:

Mindful Breathing

Take a few moments to focus on your breath. Notice the sensation of each inhale and exhale. This simple practice can help ground you in the present moment, calming your mind and bringing a sense of focus.

Mindful Walking

As you walk, pay attention to the sensations of your feet on the ground, the movement of your body, and the sights and sounds of your surroundings. This focused awareness can help you become more present in your everyday activities.

Mindful Observation

Take a moment to see your surroundings. Notice the details, the colors, the textures, and the sounds of your environment. This focused attention can help you appreciate the simple beauty of the present moment.

Mindfulness as a Spiritual Practice

Elegance embodies simplicity. Mindfulness encourages you to strip away distractions and focus on what truly matters, leading to a more elegant and graceful way of living. This clarity can help you prioritize your spiritual life and the values that reflect your faith.

Mindfulness encourages being present in the moment, which can deepen your awareness of God's presence in your life. By cultivating mindfulness, you can experience greater connection with the divine in everyday moments.

Taking time to reflect, meditate, or pray mindfully allows you to listen for divine guidance and cultivate a deeper relationship with God.

Mindfulness encourages you to notice the beauty in your surroundings. Recognizing God's handiwork in nature and every day.

Mindful Listening

When engaging in conversation, give your full attention to the speaker. Listen attentively to their words, their tone, and their body language. This active listening will not only show respect but also allow you to truly understand and connect with the other person.

Mindful Reflection

Take some time to reflect on your experiences. Consider your thoughts, your feelings, and your actions. This mindful reflection can help you gain a better understanding of yourself and cultivate a more refined and elegant approach to life.

Cultivating mindful presence is an ongoing process, a lifelong journey of self-discovery and refinement. It's about becoming more aware of yourself, your surroundings, and the interconnectedness of all things. By embracing mindful presence, you create a foundation for a more elegant, fulfilling, and meaningful life. You develop a heightened sensitivity to the world around you, enriching your experiences and allowing you to navigate social interactions with grace and confidence. Mindful presence is a powerful tool for self-improvement, enabling you to cultivate a more refined demeanor, a greater sense of inner peace, and a profound appreciation for the beauty of life.

Just as cultivating a mindful presence allows us to fully appreciate the beauty around us, it also invites us to express our individuality and creativity through the art of style and fashion.

In the next chapter, we will explore another facet of elegance: the enduring principles of timeless style and fashion that elevate our personal expression and leave a lasting impression.

"Timeless style is a philosophy, a way of approaching fashion with intention and discernment." – Gina Judy

5

TIMELESS STYLE AND FASHION

Fashion is often caught up in fleeting trends, but true elegance lies in classic pieces and lasting design principles. Timeless style is not about chasing fads, but embracing quality, craftsmanship, and design that withstand the test of time. Think of a perfectly tailored suit or a timeless trench coat, both exuding sophistication and practicality. These are the trademarks of timeless elegance, quality, and sophistication rather than short-lived trends.

The essence of timeless style lies in its ability to adapt and evolve, a graceful chameleon that seamlessly navigates the ever-changing landscape of fashion. A classic silk scarf, for instance, can transform a simple outfit from mundane to magnificent, adding a touch of understated glamour that elevates the entire ensemble. Similarly, a statement jewelry piece—a pearl necklace, a delicate pendant, or a pair of elegant earrings—can instantly elevate any look, adding a touch of timeless elegance that transcends the boundaries of trends.

Investing in timeless pieces is an investment in quality, craftsmanship, and longevity. A well-made cashmere sweater, for instance, will provide years of wear and comfort, its luxurious feel and impeccable drape a constant reminder of the enduring appeal of classic style. Similarly, a leather handbag, meticulously crafted from the finest materials, will age gracefully, developing a rich patina that only enhances its allure with time. These are not merely garments; they are enduring companions, their quality and elegance woven into the fabric of our lives.

But timeless style is more than just a collection of clothes; it's a philosophy, a way of approaching fashion with intention and discernment. It's about understanding your own personal style, finding the pieces that resonate with your authentic self, and building a wardrobe that reflects your unique sense of elegance. It's about investing in quality over quantity, choosing pieces that will stand the test of time rather than succumbing to the allure of fleeting trends.

It's a subtle art, this pursuit of timeless style—a constant dialogue between personal expression and the enduring principles of design. It's about embracing the classics while injecting them with your own unique personality, creating a wardrobe that is both timeless and uniquely yours. It's about understanding that elegance is not a destination, but a journey—a constant exploration of style, refinement, and the enduring power of quality.

And as we navigate the ever-changing landscape of fashion, let us remember that true elegance lies not in chasing the latest trends, but in embracing the enduring beauty of timeless style—a style that transcends the whims of the moment, whispering of quality, sophistication, and enduring beauty. Let us be architects of our own wardrobes, curating collections that speak to our authentic selves, and embracing the timeless elegance that lies within each carefully chosen piece.

The pursuit of elegance often involves a quest for balance and harmony. It's about finding a sweet spot between extravagance and simplicity, and in the world of fashion, few concepts embody this balance as beautifully as minimalism. Minimalist fashion isn't about stripping away all adornment; it's about a thoughtful approach to style that emphasizes clean lines, understated details, and the power of high-quality materials. It's about creating outfits that are timeless, versatile, and undeniably elegant.

Imagine a crisp white linen shirt, its fabric smooth and wrinkle-free, its cut tailored to perfection. No unnecessary embellishments, just the pure essence of a garment designed for comfort and sophistication. This is the spirit of minimalist fashion. It's about highlighting the beauty of simplicity, allowing the quality of the fabric and the craftsmanship of the garment to speak for themselves.

A minimalist wardrobe is like a curated art collection—each piece carefully chosen for its lasting value and its ability to be effortlessly combined with other items. Think of a classic trench coat, its timeless design transcending trends, and seasons. Or a tailored black blazer, versatile enough to be dressed up for a formal occasion or down for a casual meeting. Each garment is a statement of understated elegance, a reflection of a discerning eye and a commitment to quality.

The key to minimalist fashion lies in the details. It's about choosing fabrics that drape beautifully, feel luxurious against the skin, and resist the test of time. Natural fibers like silk, cotton, and wool have a timeless elegance that synthetic fabrics often lack. The focus is on quality over quantity, investing in pieces that will be cherished for years to come.

This approach extends beyond individual garments to the overall silhouette. Minimalist fashion embraces clean lines and effortless shapes, avoiding fussy details or overwhelming embellishments. A well-tailored dress with a simple A-line silhouette can be incredibly chic, while a pair of tailored trousers can be as elegant as a flowing gown. The emphasis is on creating a harmonious and refined look that's free from distractions.

Minimalism in fashion isn't about sacrificing individuality; it's about expressing your personal style in a more refined and understated way. It's about embracing the beauty of simplicity and allowing your confidence to shine through. A well-chosen minimalist outfit can be as powerful as a bold statement piece, conveying elegance, sophistication, and a quiet sense of self-assurance.

Imagine yourself walking into a room, confidently carrying yourself in a sleek black dress, its simple lines accentuated by a delicate silver necklace. You don't need a whirlwind of colors or a symphony of embellishments to make a statement; the quality of your attire and the confidence in your stride are enough to captivate attention. This is the power of minimalist fashion, a style that speaks volumes without saying a word.

Minimalism in fashion is a timeless art form, and its appeal lies in its ability to transcend trends and seasons. While fashion trends come and go, the principles of minimalism remain constant. It's about investing in quality, prioritizing comfort, and embracing simplicity. It's about creating a wardrobe that reflects your own unique sense of style, not the dictates of fleeting trends.

Think of the elegance of a minimalist design—the stark beauty of a modern sculpture, the clean lines of a Bauhaus building, or the timeless appeal of a Japanese garden. Minimalism in fashion evokes the same sense of simplicity, beauty, and enduring appeal. It's a style that speaks to a discerning eye and a refined sense of self.

So, if you're looking to cultivate a more elegant wardrobe, consider embracing the principles of minimalist fashion. It's a path to effortless sophistication, timeless style, and an undeniable sense of personal empowerment. Embrace the power of simplicity and let your true elegance shine through.

The Little Black Dress

The little black dress, a simple garment, holds a profound place in the history of fashion and continues to captivate the world with its enduring appeal. Its story, intricately interwoven with social change, artistic movements, and the evolution of women's roles, is a testament to the power of a well-crafted design to transcend generations and redefine elegance.

The origins of the little black dress can be traced back to the early 20th century, a time of significant social upheaval. The rise of women's suffrage, the burgeoning Art Deco movement, and the burgeoning film industry paved the way for a shift in fashion that favored simpler, more streamlined silhouettes. The dress, with its effortless elegance, became a symbol of modernity, a departure from the elaborate and restrictive gowns of the Victorian era.

Coco Chanel, the legendary French designer, played a pivotal role in popularizing the little black dress. In the 1920s, she introduced a simple, knee-length frock that defied traditional notions of femininity. This revolutionary design, devoid of excessive embellishments and characterized by its sleek, understated form, became a cornerstone of

Chanel's signature style. It offered women a sense of liberation, allowing them to move freely and express their individuality with ease.

The little black dress's ascent to iconic status continued through the 1950s, thanks to the Hollywood film industry. Audrey Hepburn, a cinematic icon known for her effortless grace and sophisticated charm, made the little black dress a symbol of timeless elegance in films like "Breakfast at Tiffany's." Her portrayal of Holly Golightly, a charismatic and independent character, cemented the dress's association with a sense of effortless chic and enduring appeal.

The little black dress's ability to transcend generations and adapt to changing fashion trends lies in its timeless qualities. Its simplicity allows for endless possibilities in terms of styling, from casual chic to formal elegance. The dress can be dressed up or down, paired with a statement necklace, a bold scarf, or a delicate pair of earrings. It can be layered with a blazer for a sophisticated workwear ensemble or styled with a pair of flats for a casual lunch date.

The little black dress's adaptability extends beyond its styling possibilities. It serves as a blank canvas for individual expression, allowing each wearer to infuse it with their own personality and style. Whether it's a classic A-line silhouette, a sleek sheath dress, or a flowing maxi, the little black dress embodies a universal sense of elegance that resonates with individuals from diverse backgrounds and cultures.

The little black dress's enduring appeal is further amplified by its ability to convey a sense of confidence and empowerment. In an era where women are increasingly embracing their individuality, the dress stands as a symbol of self-assurance and effortless style. Its simplicity and versatility allow women to focus on expressing their unique personalities, rather than conforming to restrictive fashion trends.

The little black dress is not the only garment that has achieved iconic status. Other timeless pieces, each with their own unique history and enduring appeal, have left an indelible mark on the fashion world. The trench coat, a practical and stylish outerwear choice, emerged in the early 20th century as a necessity for soldiers fighting in World War I. Its utilitarian design, with its distinctive buckle closure, was later adopted by civilians, becoming a staple of both men's and women's wardrobes.

The Trench Coat

Since its introduction in the early 20th century, a sleek trench coat has remained a stylish and sensible outerwear choice. Traditionally it features a double-breasted front, belted waist, and epaulettes – and is made of gabardine, cotton, or wool. It can be dressed up with tailored outfits or work over more casual attire.

Elegance icon, Audrey Hepburn, is often associated with the trench coat due to her style and memorable roles in classic films, particularly "Breakfast at Tiffany's" and "Sabrina." In "Sabrina," Audrey's character, Sabrina Fairchild, wears a stylish trench coat that adds to her sophisticated persona as she transitions from a girl-next-door to a glamorous woman. The coat is both practical and stylish, perfectly fitting her character's journey.

The trench coat's blend of functionality, history, and timeless design has secured its place as a classic and elegant wardrobe staple.

The Classic White Shirt

The classic white t-shirt, a simple yet versatile garment, has its roots in the early 20th century, initially designed for the military and laborers. Its humble beginnings transformed into a timeless fashion essential, embraced by both men and women for its comfort, practicality, and effortless style. The t-shirt's ability to be styled with everything from jeans and skirts to tailored trousers and blazers highlights its enduring appeal and versatility.

The white button-down shirt, another timeless piece, has been a staple of men's wardrobes for centuries, evolving from its origins as a practical undergarment to a versatile and stylish choice. Its clean lines, crisp texture, and timeless design have made it a staple of both formal and casual wear, adaptable to various occasions and styles. The white button-down shirt has also found its way into women's wardrobes, becoming a versatile piece that can be styled in countless ways, from tucked-in with tailored trousers to layered over a simple dress.

Due to their versatility and timeless appeal, both the classic white t-shirt and the structured white button-down shirt serve as key pieces of an elegant woman's wardrobe. It is important, however, to maintain these pieces and replace them as they become worn or discolored. Nothing ruins the polished appearance of an outfit faster than a dingy white shirt or a shirt that loses its shape. Even high-quality white shirts will lose their sharp, crisp appearance faster than darker shades. To extend their life, consider professional cleaning and oxygen bleach if necessary. Frequent replacement is also advised.

A Pair of Black Pants

Audrey Hepburn's affinity for sleek black pants embodies a timeless elegance that resonates with classic chic. Hepburn's signature looks, especially in films like "Breakfast at Tiffany's" highlighted the enduring appeal of classic pieces. Black pants go with everything and are eternally stylish. The color black has a universally flattering effect, often perceived as slimming and elongating. This quality enhances the overall silhouette, contributing to a polished and refined appearance.

Sleek black pants exemplify a minimalist style. They are clean, uncluttered, appear sophisticated, and are often associated with elegance. Whether it is a relaxed weekend or a chic social event, a sharp pair of black pants are perfect for most occasions. Dress them up with a tailored blouse and heels for evening or dress them down with a simple top and flats for a more casual look.

Incorporating sleek black pants into your wardrobe is a simple way to add a touch of sophistication and style.

The Blue Jean

The blue jean, a symbol of American ingenuity and casual chic, has a rich history that dates back to the 19th century. Originally designed as durable workwear for miners and laborers, jeans quickly became a staple of American culture, embodying a sense of rugged individualism and practicality. Blue jeans are synonymous with American fashion, culture, and have become a symbol of youth, rebellion, and individuality. They are associated with Jackie Kennedy Onassis, Katharine Hepburn, Marilyn Monroe, Audrey Hepburn, Kate Middleton and designer, Ralph Lauren.

Jackie showed us that white jeans could look quietly sophisticated. She favored ankle skimming white jeans for visits to the Cape or a day of shopping at local boutiques. Jackie paired body conscious white jeans with a black cashmere sweater for a timeless style. The stark contrast is timeless and sophisticated. The high-contrast pairing is visually striking and creates a clean, polished appearance.

While worn jeans tend to fall in the "not elegant" category, a pair of ripped jeans moved to a "relaxed elegant" status on Meghan Markle when she made her first appearance with Prince Harry at the 2017 Invictus Games. The decision to match the worn and faded jeans with a classic relaxed white button-down shirt was daring and fashionable. One of the features of Markle's fashion statement for the day included a pair of dark sunglasses. The combination of the white shirt, the relaxed jeans, and the large sunglasses worked beautifully.

While Markle's look had a relaxed elegant feel, elegance requires much more than clothing choices. In a 2024 article written by Saundra Latham, the author reveals the Duchess scored a relatively low 43% approval rating. Such a low approval rating suggests there may be other factors about the Duchess that could be perceived as less-than-elegant. Regardless of the reasons some people view Markle unfavorably, it is a good reminder that elegance is about more than the clothes you wear or the way you style them.

Looking elegant in jeans begins with a pair of jeans that fit. Slim straight jeans are meant to fit close to the body. Wearing jeans that are too big or too small can make you appear sloppy or heavy. Jeans that are too loose in the thighs and through the knees can make you appear heavy.

It is common for a woman to fluctuate in size a bit. I certainly do. As a result, I have a couple of sizes of my favorite jeans in my closet to ensure a great fit. Consider keeping two sizes of your favorite style to guarantee a perfect fit.

A great fitting pair of blue jeans is the most important style must of the elegant French woman. There's no denying that French women have a certain je ne sais quoi when it comes to their fashion sense. And when it comes to wearing jeans, they have mastered the skill. Unlike many American women who opt for skinny or distressed jeans, French women tend to stick to neutral, classic washes that are more versatile and timeless. Their jeans are also usually tailored to fit them perfectly, emphasizing the importance of a flattering, well-fitted bottom. But what's even more remarkable is how effortlessly French women can make a simple pair of jeans look chic and put-together.

During a visit to Paris, France I recall a certain French woman at a little sidewalk cafe that seemed to stand out from the crowd. Her effortless and chic style caught my attention and the attention of others around her, at least the attention of the tourists. She exuded confidence and sophistication as she sat at the quaint outdoor table, sipping a demitasse cup. Her perfectly fitted blue jeans hugged her curves in all the right places, accentuating her slender legs. But it was not just her jeans that caught the eye, it was her elegant black turtleneck that added a touch of class to her ensemble. The high neckline emphasized her slender neck and framed her delicate features. The fabric clung to her body, showing off her feminine figure. The black color also added a hint of mystery to her overall look. Completing her outfit were a pair of black high heel pump shoes, large dark Givenchy sunglasses with silver accents, a medium-sized black leather Givenchy satchel with a silver-tone lock dangling down the front and glistening earrings highlighting her sharp cheekbones. As she crossed her legs, the soles of her shoes were barely noticeable. There was an absence of red or any other bright color on the soles of her shoes. The consistent neutral tone elevated the look and ensured a level of sophistication that can sometimes be lost when pops of red color on the sole of a shoe distract you from the beauty of the person.

The heels elongated her legs, giving her a graceful and confident posture. But it wasn't just her impeccable style that made her stand out, it was the way she carried herself. With every sip, she exuded poise and grace, making the onlookers envious of her effortless elegance. As the breeze played with her hair, she smiled at the passersby, radiating warmth and charm. She was the epitome of an elegant French lady – effortlessly stylish, confident, and alluring. The little cafe seemed to come alive with her presence, and as she stood to leave, all eyes followed her.

She left a lasting impression, and I couldn't help but wonder who she was and where she was going. She was a mystery, a fashion icon, and an inspiration. As she disappeared in the bustling streets of Paris, she left behind a lingering feeling of elegance and sophistication, making the bistro a little more charming than before.

This image sticks with me. It reminds me that perfectly tailored jeans can look sharp and polished as well as relaxed and effortless. Pairing well-fitted jeans with a partially tucked-in white button-down shirt, for example, is an easy style when paired with comfortable flats or white tennis shoes. French women have a certain panache for looking stylish and confident. They have mastered the art of dressing for their bodies, rather than trying to fit into a certain size or trend. They know that true style is not about the number on the tag, but how you wear it.

The enduring appeal of blue (or black or white) jeans lies in their versatility, comfort, and timeless style, making them a fashion staple that transcends generations and continues to inspire designers and fashion enthusiasts alike.

The Cashmere Sweater

The classic cashmere sweater is considered elegant for a variety of reasons. Cashmere is a premium and high-quality material known for its softness, warmth, and luxurious feel. The fine fibers of cashmere come from the undercoat of cashmere goats, making it a rare and prized material that exudes sophistication and elegance.

Cashmere sweaters have a classic and timeless appeal that transcends trends and fads. Its simplicity and elegance make it a versatile and essential wardrobe staple.

Cashmere is prized for its exceptional softness and comfort, providing a cozy and indulgent wearing experience. The lightweight and insulating properties of cashmere make it an ideal choice for staying warm and stylish in colder weather.

Cashmere sweaters come in a variety of styles, cuts, and colors, making them versatile pieces that can be dressed up or down depending on the occasion. Whether paired with tailored trousers for a polished look or with jeans for a casual chic ensemble, a cashmere sweater adds an element of class to any outfit.

High-quality cashmere sweaters are known for their durability and longevity when properly cared for. Investing in a well-made cashmere sweater allows you to enjoy its elegance and sophistication for years to come, making it a timeless and sustainable wardrobe choice.

When I think of an elegant cashmere sweater, I think of Audrey Hepburn. Hepburn often wore classic sophisticated pieces, including cashmere sweaters, in her iconic film roles and personal style. While Hepburn wore cashmere sweaters in several of her iconic film roles, as well as her personal life, she may be most known for wearing a cashmere sweater in the classic film, "Funny Face".

In the film, Audrey's character, Jo Stockton, is often seen wearing a chic and sophisticated black cashmere turtleneck sweater, paired with tailored trousers and elegant accessories. The outfit became synonymous with Hepburn's character and is now considered an iconic and timeless fashion look. Additionally, Audrey Hepburn was known for her off-screen style, often incorporating cashmere sweaters into her personal wardrobe for a casual yet elegant look. Hepburn's love for cashmere sweaters further solidified her status as a fashion icon and symbol of timeless sophistication.

Hepburn's understated and chic aesthetic, paired with her grace and poise made her a symbol of elegance and sophistication in the fashion world. Her effortless and timeless style continues to inspire fashion trends and influence designers and fashion enthusiasts worldwide.

Or think of Kim Novak in the 1958 film, "Bell, Book, and Candle". Novak portrays the character Gillian Holroyd, a stylish and sophisticated witch living in New York City. Novak's style in the film reflected the character's enchanting and alluring personality. To reflect a contemporary and fashionable persona, Novak's character wore sleek and tailored outfits that highlighted her figure and exuded sophistication. A black cashmere turtleneck sweater was paired with black ankle skimming trousers for a stylish ensemble that blended elegance with a touch of glamour. During the film her wardrobe featured classic silhouettes in rich black cashmere and deep burgundy velvet. This color scheme also added to the character's sleek and sophisticated aesthetic.

I personally love a fitted black cashmere turtleneck sweater with figure flattering white jeans or high-quality white shorts. Pairing this classic color duo with a nice pair of large black sunglasses is undoubtedly a head turner. When a turtleneck seems a bit too heavy for the season, shift to a cashmere boatneck sweater in a neutral color.

The boatneck style, also known as a bateau neckline, follows the natural curve of the collarbone and shoulders, creating an elegant and elongated neckline. This neckline style draws attention to the shoulders and collarbone, which are typically flattering areas on most body types.

The boatneck sweater's wide and horizontal neckline visually broadens the shoulders and balances out the proportions of the upper body. This can create a more symmetrical and proportionate silhouette, especially for individuals with narrower shoulders or a smaller bust. The wide neckline can create a slimming effect by drawing the eye upwards and elongating the neck. This helps create a vertical line that visually lengthens the torso and enhances the overall appearance of the body.

Due to its luxurious material, timeless style, exceptional comfort, versatility, and durability, a well fitted cashmere sweater is a perfect addition to any woman's wardrobe. It is a classic and sophisticated wardrobe staple that adds a touch of luxury and refinement to any outfit, making it a symbol of elegance and style.

The Tailored Blazer

The tailored blazer is another essential part of any elegant wardrobe, offering a polished and refined finish to any ensemble. Its structured silhouette instantly elevates a look, providing a sense of power and sophistication. A well-tailored blazer is an indispensable piece, one that can be effortlessly styled in countless ways. Whether paired with tailored trousers for a powerful statement or draped over a structured dress, the tailored blazer is a chameleon, adapting to the wearer's unique style and personality.

The timeless appeal of a classic blazer lies in its ability to transcend trends and seasons. Its versatility is unparalleled, allowing it to be dressed up or down with effortless ease. For a casual daytime look, layer it over a simple tee, pairing it with distressed jeans and sneakers for an air of relaxed elegance. Alternatively, for a more formal affair, style it with a sleek pencil skirt and heels, adding a touch of glamour with statement jewelry. The possibilities are endless, ensuring the blazer's status as a wardrobe staple that adapts to the ever-evolving fashion landscape. The key to the blazer's enduring popularity is its ability to empower the wearer. Its structured shoulders and nipped-in waist create a powerful silhouette, exuding confidence, and a sense of authority.

A longer blazer or structured coat worn over the shoulders of an outfit in a matching color creates a striking monochromatic silhouette that says class and refinement.

Monochromatic looks in neutral colors of gray, black, ivory, white, navy, and taupe emit an air of sophistication and places the focus on the wearer.

Duotone refers to a design technique that uses two contrasting colors to create a visually appealing effect. Sophisticated two-color combinations are:

White and Black

Navy and White

Cream and Brown

Gray and Burgundy

Mixing colors can also relay a high-quality image if a dominant neutral color is combined with no more than two other colors. This concept is often referred to as the "3 color rule". Use the "3-color rule" to coordinate a double-breasted navy blazer with white tailored slacks or jeans. Add a taupe top handle handbag and taupe high heel pumps for a sharp country-club look. In fashion, the 3-color rule is a guideline for creating visually balanced and cohesive outfits that do not bring too many colors together. The rule states that an outfit should have no more than three colors: a dominant color, a secondary color, and an accent color. The dominant color is the color reflected by the majority of the outfit. The secondary color is about one-third of the outfit, and the accent color complements the other colors.

The 3-color rule minimizes the risk of overwhelming combinations that can shift the eye away from your beauty and essence. Here are a few classic three-color combinations are:

Navy, White, Taupe

Gray, Black, White

Blue, Camel, Brown

Keep in mind, wearing bold gold tone or silver tone jewelry and hardware may serve as an accent color. The same can be true of strong hair colors and dominant hair styles. To achieve a polished and sleek look, step back from the mirror and see if you have too many competing shades taking place. If so, reduce the visual confusion by removing a color or toning one of the visual elements down.

The modern blazer dress, whether in a mini or longer length, is a business-inspired look with high-impact. The structured elements of a beautifully cut mini blazer dress in elevated suiting fabric makes it a perfect sophisticated style for a cocktail party or evening out. While this style can be found in a variety of colors, stick with neutral tones to keep the look elevated.

To ensure you achieve and maintain a high-end, timeless appearance, the blazer-dress must be impeccably cut and tailored to your measurements. A blazer dress with a low-grade fabric or a dress requiring rolled up sleeves can be too relaxed to be perceived as elevated and refined. As a result, avoid these features when considering this style.

For a smaller 5'4" frame (or under), a black blazer mini dress can take the place of the little black dress. It lengthens the leg and creates a flattering silhouette. It's a perfect opportunity to accessorize with that gorgeous vintage brooch or Chanel camellia flower. For an elevated look, add a monochromatic designer pump and a matching structured handbag.

An impeccably tailored white blazer dress is ideal for warmer weather, for a lady's luncheon, or even a rehearsal dinner option for the bride-to-be. Pair with matching or nude-tone heels and handbag. If you are a fan of hats, try a sharp little pill box or narrow brim boater in a complimentary color or texture.

The tailored blazer commands attention, conveying a message of strength and sophistication. Whether in the boardroom or at a social event, a tailored blazer adds an air of refinement, making it a staple for women who wish to assert their presence with style and grace.

The Classic Pointed-Toe Pump

Originally pointed-toe heels were worn by men in the European aristocracy. The pointed toe was a symbol of status and wealth. Catherine de Medici, Queen of France, is credited for the popularity of heels for women. On her wedding day in 1533, she wore thin heels designed to make her appear taller. Over time, the design evolved, and by the 17th century, the classic pointed-toe pump was a chic design that made its way to women's fashion.

The pump (or court shoe) refers to the type and styling of the upper portion of the shoe that does not cover the top of the foot area but does cover all or most of the toe area. The toe area has a pointed shape that serves to slim the foot and make it appear more feminine.

Its ability to instantly make a women appear more attractive is one of the main reasons it has withstood the test of time.

In its refined high heel version, the pump has the ability to give shape to a woman's calves and elongate the appearance of her legs. Pumps also increase pelvic tilt and can lift a woman's derriere by 20-30%!

In addition to the elegant look of a high heel pump on a woman, the walk of a woman in a high pump is striking. Research reveals that men perceive a woman walking in high heel pumps to be more elegant and beautiful than when she is walking in flat or chunky shoes.

Remember this the next time a bright pink chunky – block heel shoe with ankle straps turns your head. Is that shoe going to enhance or take away from your natural beauty? Is that shoe going to elongate your stride or contribute to a smooth, easy glide as you walk across the room?

To walk in a striking pointed-toe high heel pump, stand up straight with your eyes looking forward. Walk with your feet positioned straight, toes pointed forward and heels vertical to the ground. Taking small steps, place one foot in front of the other with a smooth, even stepping motion. Each step should begin at the heel and roll to the toe. In essence, walk on the balls of your feet and use the heel for balance. Keep in mind, high heels can throw you off balance. As a result, walking in heels can be difficult. When elevating your heels you will increase the amount of pressure placed on your foot. This pushes your body forward which changes your balance and the way you walk.

Train your feet to walk in heels by working your ankles, calves, and arches. You can start with lower kitten heels if you would like. With a high-quality shoe and a little practice, I am confident you will be walking beautifully in sleek pointed-toe pump heels in no time.

Whether you opt for a leg lengthening nude pump, a sophisticated black pump, or a colorful pump that accentuates a fashion choice – make high heel pumps a wardrobe staple.

Simply stated, a woman walking in a high heel pump is sensuous and feminine. No wonder it is the preferred shoe of enduring fashion icons and members of royalty.

The Structured Top Handle Bag

While a clutch handbag is sleek and an extremely elegant bag to include in your wardrobe, a high-end top handle bag is perceived as feminine, luxurious, and sophisticated. It will also withstand the test of time.

My favorite top handle bag is the Lady Dior. The Lady Dior bag is a classic and elegant style that features quilted "cannage" stitching, a top handle, and iconic Dior charms. In my opinion, it is the most timeless and refined design.

On a trip to Paris, France I had the opportunity to visit the Dior Galerie to see exhibitions that highlight Christian Dior's iconic designs. While the process of making a Lady Dior handbag is not typically open to the public for viewing, I was fortunate to observe a behind-the-scenes glimpse into the craftsmanship and artistry that goes into creating the timeless A-line handbag style.

The bag is made up of 140 pieces that are assembled around a wooden form. It is quilted using 1,500 stitches to create the "cannage" pattern. The pattern is inspired by the Napoleon III chairs that Christian Dior used to seat guests at his runway shows. The Lady Dior bag features gold or silver tone D-I-O-R letters and the Dior logo suspended from the handle as charms. Charms, such as these, act as a Dior signature as they remind us of the lucky charms Christian Dior tended to carry.

While the bag was first introduced in 1994 as the Chouchou bag, it became known as the Lady Dior in 1995 after it became a favorite design of Lady Diana. Lady Diana loved the bag and was spotted carrying it often.

Chanel's Classic Flap Bag is another favorite timeless handbag style that can be worn as a top handle or cross body. This quilted bag with the signature CC logo exudes sophistication and is a must have for many fashion enthusiasts.

The Hermes Birkin was first launched in 1984 as a utilitarian and trendsetting handbag inspired by It-girl Jane Birkin. Known for its impeccable craftsmanship, premium materials, and timeless design, the Birkin is a symbol of status and sophistication. The bag features two rolled handles, top flaps with buckle loops and a lock and key. It is one of the most coveted and luxurious handbags in the world.

Hermes only produces a limited number each year and the styles are often kept secret. Hermes boutiques are only able to obtain a select number of the Birkin every 6 months, so the bags are very exclusive and can require exceptionally long wait times. For these reasons, the Hermes Birkin bag tops the list of the most expensive handbags. As the bags tend to retain or increase in value, approximately 25% of Birkin owners keep their bags in storage for future resale.

Other notable mentions are the Louis Vuitton Alma bag, the Gucci Jackie Bag (also known as the Gucci Ophidia), and the Celine Luggage Tote.

These luxury handbags are some of the most elegant handbags that have stood the test of time and remain highly sought after in the world of fashion. Each of these handbags exudes sophistication, luxury, and timeless elegance, making them classic choices for your wardrobe.

The Power of a Hat

Hats can evoke a sense of elegance and sophistication. Hats can also add flair and personality to an outfit. They can enhance an overall look, making it appear more polished and put-together.

A well-chosen hat can beautifully frame a woman's face, highlighting her features and drawing attention in a flattering way. This can enhance her overall appearance and contribute to a more graceful look.

Wearing a hat gives a sense of confidence and poise. The act of wearing something distinctive can make someone feel more self-assured and stylish. A hat has the power to elevate an outfit by providing a focal point and adding a layer of visual interest.

There are countless styles of hats, from wide-brimmed sun hats and elegant fascinators to chic berets and stylish fedoras. Each style can convey a different mood or message, allowing women to express their individuality and taste.

When choosing a hat, consider your face shape to find a style that complements your features. Here are some suggestions for the best hat styles for different face shapes:

Round Face

If you have a round face shape, opt for hats with angular or structured designs to add some definition and elongate your face. Fedoras or wide brim hats with a slight tilt can help create the illusion of a longer face.

Square Face

Soft and rounded hat styles work best with a square shaped face as they balance out angular features. Floppy hats, cloche hats, slouchy beanies, or round crown hats are best to try as they can soften the lines of your face.

Oval Face

Lucky you! An oval face shape is considered the most versatile and can pull off almost any hat style. Experiment with different shapes like cloche hats, berets, pillbox, bucket hats, and fedoras to find what suits you best.

Long Face

To complement a long face shape, choose a hat that adds width and volume to the sides of your face. Cloche hats, beanies, berets, and wide brim hats can frame the face in a way that may make it appear shorter or more rounded.

Heart-shaped Face

If you have a heart-shaped face with a wider forehead and a narrower chin, opt for hats that add width to the lower part of your face. Floppy hats, fedoras with a wider brim, or wide-brim sun hats can help balance out your features.

Ultimately, the best hat for your face shape is one that makes you feel confident and comfortable. Experiment with different styles and don't be afraid to step out of your comfort zones to find the perfect hat that suits your features and personal style.

The Hermes Scarf

The Hermes scarf. You can spot it a mile away.

These scarves are made from high-quality silk, which is known for its softness, luster, and durability. The silk used in Hermes scarves is often sourced from the best silk and crafted by skilled artisans in France. The process for creating a Hermes scarf involves numerous steps, including designing, printing, and hand finishing. Timeless and elegant patterns make the scarves versatile and suitable for a variety of occasions. This attention to detail and craftsmanship contribute to its high-quality.

Even though the House of Hermes has been located in Paris, France since the 19th century, the Hermes scarf can be seen on beautiful, stylish women throughout Italy. These sophisticated women exude elegance and confidence as they effortlessly incorporate the luxurious silk scarf into their outfits. Whether they are strolling through the streets of Milan or sipping espresso at a chic café in Rome, the Hermes scarf is a staple accessory for the fashionable Italian woman. It adds a touch of refinement and sophistication to any ensemble, elevating it to a whole new level.

The way these women delicately handle the silk scarf, carefully tying it in a knot or letting it flow freely in the breeze, is a true testament to their impeccable taste and style. It's no wonder that the Hermes scarf has become a symbol of high fashion and is coveted by women all over the world.

Throughout Europe it is common to catch a glimpse of a Hermes Twilly tied around the handle of a structured satchel or wrapped around the wrist next to a luxury timepiece. The Twilly looks particularly polished and sharp when positioned around your neck as a compliment to a classic shirt or blazer.

A square Hermes 90 is a favorite of women vacationing on the Mediterranean as the silk is excellent for keeping all types of hair frizz-free. This 34.8" X 34.8" scarf is also an ideal size to wear around the neck in dozens of ways.

A silk scarf from the prestigious fashion house, Hermes, is a little piece of luxury that will not only elevate your style but will also add a touch of elegance and sophistication to any outfit.

Dark Sunglasses

Dark sunglasses have a classic and timeless appearance that transcends trends and fads. The simple and understated design of dark sunglasses adds a touch of sophistication and elegance to any outfit. They are a versatile accessory that can be paired with a wide range of outfits, from casual to formal. Their neutral color and sleek design make them suitable for various occasions and styles. There is also a mysterious and alluring quality about dark sunglasses that can create a sense of intrigue and sophistication. The dark lenses have a slimming effect on the face and add an element of mystery to the wearer's appearance, enhancing their overall allure.

Jackie Kennedy Onassis, often referred to as Jackie O, was known for her elegance and iconic sense of style, which included her frequent wearing of dark sunglasses. She was often photographed outdoors, and wearing sunglasses helped protect her eyes from the sun's rays while maintaining her glamorous appearance. As a public figure she garnered significant attention and scrutiny from the media and the public. By wearing dark sunglasses, she was able to shield her eyes and maintain a level of privacy and anonymity in public settings. The sunglasses added an air of mystery and intrigue to her persona, allowing her to navigate public spaces with a sense of discretion.

Chanel, Tom Ford, Cartier, Prada, and Dior are known for stylish sunglasses in all shapes and sizes. If you are seeking a touch of glamour, explore Italian designer, Sospiri. Each pair of Sospiri sunglasses features a touch of Swarovski sparkle.

In recent years there has been a resurgence of classic-style sunglass shapes. Classic cat eye, aviators, oversized frames, and square shapes tend to fit a variety of face shapes and possess an enduring appeal.

When investing in a high-quality pair of dark sunglasses to elevate your wardrobe, handle them with care to prevent scratches and prolong the life of the eyewear. Avoid placing them face down on hard surfaces so they do not scratch. Place them lens-side up or lay them on their side or store them in a protective case to minimize damage. While high quality sunglasses are often sold with a protective case, if the case is too large or bulky you may consider purchasing a smaller or cloth case as a back-up option to accommodate smaller handbags. Soft sided, cloth sunglass cases are also perfect gifts for friends. You can usually find extra cloth sunglass cases at a local boutique or through Amazon.

Part of the overall look and feel of an elegant woman includes impeccable grooming. This includes your accessories, like sunglasses. Keep a microfiber cleaning cloth or an individual packet of lens cleaner available in the sunglass case to remove dirt, dust, and smudges.

The Cartier Tank Watch

While we are considering the elegant style of Jackie O, let's discuss the other timeless accessory that can elevate your style: The classic tank watch. Jackie O was frequently seen wearing a tank watch as part of her signature look. The tank watch is a classic and sophisticated timepiece known for its rectangular shape and sleek design, which complimented Jackie O's chic and understated style. Her choice to wear a tank watch further solidified her status as a fashion icon and trendsetter, and the watch became synonymous with her classic and elegant aesthetic.

Specifically, Jackie O preferred Cartier's version of the tank watch. Other famous fans include Princess Diana, Audrey Hepburn, Cary Grant, and Clark Gable. All individuals known for an elegant, sophisticated aesthetic.

Cartier created the Tank watch in 1917. The watch was inspired by the shape of World War I tanks, which were newly introduced vehicles of the time. Since its inception over a century ago, the Cartier Tank watch continues to be a symbol of luxury, sophistication, and timeless style.

It is such a popular timepiece that Cartier has created several variations. Over the years, Cartier developed different models and collections within the Tank watch line, each with its own unique design features and characteristics.

These iconic pieces, each with their own unique story and lasting appeal, have shaped the world of fashion, offering timeless elegance and style that transcends generations and cultural boundaries. They stand as reminders of the power of well-crafted designs to endure, inspire, and empower individuals to express their unique personalities and embrace the enduring allure of timeless elegance.

Diamond Stud Earrings

Diamond stud earrings are often considered a quintessential piece of jewelry due to their timeless elegance and versatility. Diamonds are traditionally associated with luxury and wealth. Wearing diamond studs can elevate one's appearance and convey a sense of affluence and sophistication.

Diamonds are known for their exceptional brilliance and sparkle. The way they catch and reflect light adds a touch of glamour and sophistication. They frame the face beautifully, enhancing an individual's features without drawing attention away from them.

Their minimalist design exudes understated elegance. Whether it's a day at the office or an elegant evening out, their simplicity complements any outfit without overwhelming the overall look.

Diamond stud earrings come in various shapes, sizes, and settings. Whether opting for a larger statement-making pair or a delicate smaller pair, there's a diamond stud for everyone.

The Art of Dressing Appropriately

The ability to dress appropriately for various occasions is a cornerstone of elegance. It's not about following the latest trends or wearing the most expensive clothes; it's about understanding the unspoken language of fashion and using it to communicate respect for the setting and the people involved. Imagine a formal dinner party. Would you wear a pair of ripped jeans and a t-shirt to such an event? The answer is a resounding no. Why? Because your attire would clash with the formality of the occasion, signaling a lack of consideration for the hosts and other guests. Similarly, attending a casual gathering in a tuxedo would feel out of place, creating an air of awkwardness and possibly even offense.

Dressing appropriately is a delicate balance between expressing your personal style and respecting the context of the event. It's about recognizing the subtle cues that indicate the level of formality, the mood, and the purpose of the occasion. Consider a business meeting. While a well-tailored suit or sophisticated dress might be appropriate for a high-level executive meeting, a more relaxed approach with polished casual wear might be suitable for a brainstorming session with colleagues. The key is to understand the specific requirements of the event and choose an outfit that aligns with the expectations without sacrificing your own sense of style.

The art of dressing appropriately is not limited to formal occasions. It extends to everyday interactions, from a visit to the grocery store to a date night with your partner. A casual outfit, chosen with care, can still convey a sense of elegance. Think clean lines, well-fitting garments, and classic pieces that reflect your personal style. Even a simple t-shirt can be elevated with the right jeans, a stylish scarf, and a pair of polished shoes. It's about paying attention to details, from the fit of your clothing to the accessories you choose and ensuring that your attire reflects a sense of personal care and respect for the occasion.

The importance of appropriateness extends beyond the individual's own appearance. It's about recognizing the impact your attire has on others. When you dress appropriately, you create a sense of harmony and respect, fostering a positive and comfortable atmosphere. You send a silent message that you value the event, the people involved, and the shared experience.

For those who might find it challenging to navigate the complexities of appropriate attire, remember the key lies in understanding the context. Do your research, ask for guidance when needed, and, most importantly, trust your instincts. When in doubt, err on the side of formality. It's better to be slightly overdressed than underdressed, especially when attending a special occasion.

Elegance is not about conforming to rigid rules; it's about embracing the principles of respect, consideration, and appropriateness. It's about understanding that clothing is a form of communication, a way of expressing your personality and your respect for the occasion and the people you are with. Embrace this language of fashion, and you will unlock a world of elegance, where style becomes a powerful tool for forging connections, creating memorable experiences, and expressing your authentic self.

Accessories

Accessories, those seemingly small details, possess an extraordinary power to elevate an outfit from ordinary to extraordinary. They act as the exclamation point to a well-crafted sentence, adding a touch of individuality, personality, and sophistication. Think of a beautifully tailored suit—it's a masterpiece in itself but imagine the impact of a silk scarf cascading down the back, or a vintage brooch gleaming on the lapel, a statement of elegance in miniature. The right accessory can transform a simple dress into an evening ensemble, infusing it with a touch of drama and refinement. It's an art, a subtle dance between contrast and harmony, where the right piece enhances, complements, and elevates the entire ensemble.

But how to navigate this intricate world of accessorizing? The key, as with all aspects of elegance, lies in understanding the nuances of balance and subtlety. It's about choosing pieces that resonate with your personal style, accentuate your best features, and add a touch of sophistication without overwhelming the outfit. The focus should always be on enhancing, not overpowering. A simple, well-chosen piece, whether it's a statement necklace, a pair of bold earrings, or a sleek watch, can elevate a look, but it's the careful curation of these elements that elevates the overall aesthetic.

Let's consider a classic example: the little black dress. A timeless piece, it can effortlessly transform from a simple day outfit to a chic evening ensemble depending on the accessories. A bold statement necklace with dramatic geometric shapes can make the dress perfect for a cocktail party. A delicate gold chain with a pendant, on the other hand, adds a touch of elegance for a casual lunch date. Paired with bright, bold earrings, the little black dress becomes a conversation starter, while sleek, simple earrings create a more understated and sophisticated look. Each choice, each accessory, tells a story, adding a layer of complexity and individual flair to the timeless silhouette.

The world of accessories is a treasure trove of possibilities, each piece whispering a tale of history, culture, and personal expression. A vintage brooch, with its intricate details and stories woven into its design, speaks of a bygone era, adding a touch of vintage charm to a modern ensemble. A hand-woven scarf, its intricate patterns reflecting the artistry of a skilled artisan, adds a touch of cultural richness to a simple outfit. The choices you make, the accessories you select, reveal not just your taste but your personality, your story.

Choosing accessories that complement your personal style is paramount. If your aesthetic leans towards minimalist, then understated pieces like a delicate chain necklace, a sleek watch, or a simple bracelet will be your best friends. They add a touch of refinement without detracting from the clean lines of your outfit. If your style is bolder and more expressive, consider statement pieces – a chunky necklace with colorful gemstones, a pair of vibrant earrings, or a statement ring. These pieces, like punctuation marks, emphasize your personality and make a statement.

But the art of accessorizing transcends mere aesthetics. It's about understanding the context, the occasion, and the message you wish to convey. A classic black-tie event calls for elegant pieces that complement the formality of the occasion – pearls, a sleek clutch, or a simple but refined watch. A casual lunch date, on the other hand, allows for a more relaxed approach, incorporating pieces that reflect your personal style, whether it's a bohemian scarf, a colorful bracelet, or a fun pair of earrings. The key is to strike a balance, choosing pieces that enhance the occasion without being overly flashy or distracting.

Here are some tips for choosing the perfect accessories:

Consider the Occasion

The formality of the event dictates the type of accessories you choose. A casual gathering allows for more playful and expressive pieces, while formal events require refined and understated choices.

Reflect Your Personal Style

Your accessories should reflect your unique personality and taste. Don't be afraid to experiment and find pieces that resonate with your aesthetic.

Embrace Color and Texture

Use color and texture to add visual interest to your outfit. A pop of color can brighten a neutral ensemble, while textured fabrics like velvet or silk add a touch of luxury.

Pay Attention to Proportion

Choose accessories that are proportionate to your body and the outfit. Too many accessories can create a cluttered look, while too few may make the outfit seem incomplete.

Invest in Quality Pieces

Seek out well-crafted accessories that are durable and timeless. A high-quality piece, like a classic leather handbag or a statement ring, will last for years to come.

Ultimately, accessorizing is an art form, a way to express your individuality and elevate your personal style. It's about finding the perfect balance, the harmonious interplay of details that creates a cohesive and refined look. It's about making a statement, not with a loud voice, but with a whisper of elegance, a touch of sophistication, and a dash of your unique personality.

A Neutral Color Palette

An elegant style is often associated with neutral colors, which have a versatile and sophisticated look, making them easy to mix and match. The color palette used in a refined style typically includes black, white, navy, gray, cream, taupe and beige. These colors are timeless and classic, providing a sense of luxury and elegance to any outfit. They are also perfect for creating a polished and put-together look, without being too bold or flashy.

In addition to being versatile and easy to match, neutral colors also have a calming and soothing effect. They create a sense of balance and harmony, making them perfect for creating a relaxed and refined style. Whether you are dressing for a formal event or a casual day out, incorporating neutral colors into your outfit can instantly elevate your look and give off an air of sophistication.

Neutral colors are not only limited to clothing, but they can also be incorporated into accessories and home decor. By using these colors in your accessories, such as shoes, bags, and jewelry, you can add a touch of elegance to any outfit. In home decor, neutral colors create a serene and tranquil atmosphere, making your living space a peaceful and inviting place. Overall, neutral colors are an essential element in creating a refined style that is timeless, classic, and sophisticated.

Wear White Year Round

The idea of not wearing white after Labor Day has its roots in American fashion in the late 19th and early 20th centuries. The practice is often attributed to the upper-class society wearing white for leisure and summer activities while taking vacations during the summer months. At that time wearing white was seen as a sign of wealth and status. Once summer ended, the wealthier classes would return to the city and dress in more formal dark colors.

Over the years, the "no white after Labor-Day" rule has relaxed. Modern fashion embraces the idea of wearing white throughout the year as long as the fabrics are seasonably appropriate. For example, a beautiful white tailored coat in the winter or a white off-shoulder boucle midi dress in the fall are very chic looks.

Tailoring

Clothing should fit well – neither too tight nor too loose. Tailored pieces that complement the body shape often contribute to a polished appearance. With this in mind, tailoring is an essential aspect of achieving a timeless and elegant look. It involves creating well-fitted clothing that is tailored to your body shape, giving you a polished and sophisticated appearance. This attention to detail and precision in tailoring can elevate any outfit, adding a touch of elegance and refinement that sets you apart.

In home decor, the use of cohesive neutral colors is key in creating a serene and tranquil atmosphere. These colors, such as beige, cream, and gray, have a calming effect and can make your living space a peaceful and inviting place. Use neutral colors with well-tailored furnishings and accents, this creates a cohesive and sophisticated look that exudes a sense of luxury. Let neutrality extend to walls, flooring, and timeless fixtures. Create a cohesive and elegant look that reflects a sense of attention to detail and refinement.

Whether you're dressing up for a special occasion or decorating your home, remember that tailoring and neutral colors are essential elements in creating a refined style that stands the test of time.

Equestrian Chic

Imagine wearing an elegant, tailored riding jacket that hugs your silhouette. The jacket's rich navy hue and sleek dark slacks complement the crisp white blouse you have chosen. A silk scarf to tie gracefully around your neck introduces a pop of color and a hint of equestrian flair. To complete your ensemble, you have added a structured leather handbag and matching belt.

It's a perfect blend of equestrian elegance and modern fashion. It's a striking image.

Equestrian style features tailored pieces, such as fitted jackets, crisp shirts, and tailored trousers, which create a polished and sophisticated look. The classic lines and silhouettes are timeless and appeal to a wide range of fashion sensibilities. The style often incorporates thoughtful details such as stitching, buttons, and hardware that add character and sophistication.

Equestrian fashion is often associated with a rich heritage and tradition, particularly in countries with a long history of horseback riding, such as England. This cultural significance lends an air of sophistication and class to the style.

Elements like riding boots, jodhpurs, tailored blazers, silk scarves, crisp white shirts, vests, leather belts, and leather handbags are fashionable choices that appeal to a wide audience and exude class and sophistication.

The timeless elegance of equestrian elements makes this style perpetually fashionable.

The French Tuck

The French tuck is a popular styling technique because it adds a touch of sophistication and visual interest to an outfit. Tucking in the front of a shirt and leaving the back of the shirt untucked gives off a relaxed and chic vibe while still looking put-together and stylish. It can also create a more defined waistline and elongate the legs.

To achieve this perfect balance between casual and polished, start by putting on a crisp button up shirt. Grab the front of the shirt and tuck it into the waistband of your pants or skirt, but only on one side. Leave the back and sides of the shirt untucked. Adjust the tuck so it is slightly loose and relaxed, rather than tightly tucked in. Smooth out any wrinkles or bunching in the fabric to create a clean finish. You can leave the rest of the shirt untucked for a casual and effortless style.

If your French tuck adds bulk when tucked in, there are a couple of secrets French women know that ensure a smooth slim appearance. The secret involves simply not tucking in so much fabric. To achieve this, begin with a crisp cotton shirt. Put the shirt on inside out and upside down. Tuck the front bottom of the shirt under your bra then pull your shirt up and put it back on so you are left with just enough shirt to just tuck it in. Next, fasten the buttons.

Another method that is a bit more complicated, but eliminates tucking in any fabric, involves rolling the shirt under and fastening the bottom button to the chest level buttonhole, and using the bottom buttonhole as the fastener for the chest level button. Finally button the top button at chest level.

Experiment with different lengths and styles of shirts to find the best way to French tuck for your body type and personal style.

An elegant style is a timeless and sophisticated approach to fashion that transcends trends and fads. It is about looking effortlessly chic and put-together, with a focus on quality, classic pieces, and attention to detail.

Attention to Detail

To achieve an elegant style, pay attention to the small details. These details, like well-groomed hair, polished shoes, and subtle accessories, may seem insignificant, but they play an important role in elevating your overall appearance.

For example, well-manicured hands and feet look more attractive. Be mindful of personal hygiene and ensure nails are clean and manicured. Regular manicures help keep nails healthy by preventing issues such as hangnails, splits, and brittleness. Many manicures include exfoliation and moisturizing of the hands, which prevents dryness and keeps the skin looking youthful and healthy. Regular pedicures help maintain foot hygiene and should include nail shaping, buffing, and painting to ensure your toenails are neat and polished. In terms of polish, opt for classic nail colors for a timeless look. A French manicure or shades that closely match your skin tone, such as beige, soft pink, or taupe, provides a polished, delicate, understated, and feminine appearance.

Clothes should be clean, free of lint, free of wrinkles, in good condition, without any visible damage or excessive wear. Shoes should be clean and in good condition, matching the overall style of the outfit. Polished shoes, whether heels or flats, also add to a refined appearance.

By attending to these details, you show that you are a person that is meticulous and that you take pride in your appearance. Not only do these small details project an elegant vibe, but they also show you are a person who values attention to detail.

An elegant style is not just about the clothes you wear, but it is about how you present your home, your office, and yourself. By focusing on the small details, you show that you are someone who takes the time to carefully curate their look, and that you have a refined sense of style.

In addition to enhancing your overall appearance, paying attention to details boosts your confidence. When you know you have put effort into every aspect of your look, you will feel more self-assured and poised. This not only elevates your look, but it makes you feel elegant.

Remember, the devil is in the details, and by paying attention to them, you can achieve an elegant style that is sure to turn heads.

In the next Chapter we will explore fragrance and the perfect invisible accessory . . . a signature scent.

"A signature scent is the subtle finishing touch . . . your invisible accessory."
– Gina Judy

6

THE ELEGANCE OF A SIGNATURE SCENT

As she glides into the room, all eyes are drawn to her effortlessly chic demeanor, and impeccable sense of style. While the clothing she selected for the day exudes sophistication and grace, it is her choice of fragrance that truly sets her apart. The luxurious perfume she wears is like an invisible accessory, complementing her every movement with an air of elegance and refinement. With each step she takes, a trail of intoxicating scent follows her, leaving a lingering impression of opulence and allure.

The fragrance, a harmonious blend of floral and citrus notes, perfectly complements her sophisticated taste and adds an extra layer of sophistication to her already impeccable ensemble. Like a whisper of luxury, her perfume is the final touch that completes her look and sets her apart as a true embodiment of timeless beauty and grace.

This is an elegant woman who understands the importance of selecting the perfect signature fragrance.

She knows a signature scent sets her apart and makes her stand out. It is a way for her to differentiate herself and leave a memorable impression on others. Her signature scent is a part of her personal identity and style. She understands when someone smells good, it automatically makes them more attractive and appealing. While this understanding may be instinctive, it has been proven in a number of studies. One study published in the journal "Psychological Science" by Hummel et al. (2012) demonstrated that individuals rated as more attractive were also perceived as smelling better. Participants in the study rated the body odor of individuals based on photographs, indicating a strong correlation between visual and olfactory cues in attractiveness. So, from a psychological perspective, smelling good automatically makes you more beautiful.

A signature scent can become a part of your personal brand and identity too. It is a way to express your personality, style, and individuality, and can leave a lasting impression on others. Scent has a powerful connection to memory and emotion. A signature scent can evoke positive memories and emotions for both you and others, creating a sense of familiarity and comfort.

Your signature scent is a unique fragrance that becomes synonymous with you, leaving a lasting impression on those around you. Just as a signature piece of jewelry or clothing can define your style, a signature scent can convey your personality and leave a lasting memory in the minds of others. Whether it's a soft floral scent, a bold and spicy fragrance, or a fresh and clean aroma, a signature scent can be a powerful tool to express your individuality and leave a lasting impact.

Wearing a signature scent that you love can boost your confidence and make you feel good about yourself. It can be a subtle yet impactful way to enhance your overall presence and self-assurance. It also provides a sense of consistency and continuity in your personal style . . . a reliable element in your daily routine, an invisible accessory that adds a touch of sophistication and refinement.

Finding your signature scent is a personal and individual process that involves understanding fragrance and discovering which fragrances resonate with your personality, style, body chemistry, environment, and preferences.

Fragrance

Perfumes have long been hailed as one of the most intimate and personal forms of self-expression, with the power to evoke memories, emotions, and even alter moods. From ancient times to the modern era, the art of perfumery has captivated and enchanted people across cultures and continents.

The intricate blend of top, heart, and base notes creates a symphony of scents that can transport us to distant lands, evoke nostalgia, or simply add a touch of luxury to our everyday lives.

The top notes of a fragrance are sometimes known as the opening notes or head notes because they are the initial impression you get when you first apply the perfume. These notes are light, fresh, and volatile, meaning they evaporate quickly. They are quick to appear and disappear. They are what you smell first and typically last for the first 15-30 minutes after application. Common top notes include citrus, fruity, and herbal scents.

The heart notes, also known as the middle notes, emerge after the top notes have dissipated. These notes make up the main body of the fragrance and provide the character and personality of the scent. They are usually floral or spicy notes that last longer than the top notes, typically lasting for several hours. They are often the most prominent and shape the fragrance's personality. They bring together the top and base notes and are often fruity, blending easily with other notes.

The base notes, also known as soul notes, are the final phase of a perfume and emerge after the heart notes have faded. These notes are the foundation of the fragrance and are typically rich, deep, and long-lasting. Base notes are what linger on the skin for hours after application and have a strong impact on the memory of the scent. Common base notes include woody, musky, and resinous scents.

The opening, heart, and base notes of a perfume are different components that make up the overall scent profile of a fragrance.

Perfume notes are also categorized by their scent, such as fresh, floral, spice, fruit, wood, and musk. The presence of one note can alter the perception of another. For example, the scent of base notes in the drydown can be altered by the smells of the heart notes.

Understanding the notes of a perfume can enhance your overall appreciation and enjoyment of the fragrance and provide you with a greater understanding of why some fragrances may be more suited to you than others. Knowing the notes in a perfume can help you make more informed choices when selecting a new fragrance. If you prefer certain scents or notes, understanding the composition of a perfume can guide you in choosing a fragrance that aligns with you – your signature scent.

Finding Your Signature Scent

Finding your signature scent can be fun and rewarding. Start by exploring different fragrance families, such as floral, exotic, woody, citrus, or fresh scents. Test a variety of perfumes to determine to which scent profiles you are drawn.

Think about the scents that you naturally gravitate toward. Do you prefer floral notes or warm and spicy scents? Do you gravitate to fresh and clean fragrances? How about sweet scents? Gourmand scents?

A gourmand scent has sweet, edible, and dessert-like notes. These scents tend to evoke indulgence and comfort, reminiscent of delicious treats and culinary delights. Gourmand scents typically feature notes such as vanilla, spices, fruits, and various baked goods. Some popular gourmand perfumes are Thierry Mugler's Angel and Prada Candy.

Bergamot is a popular ingredient in many luxury perfumes due to its fresh, citrusy, and slightly floral scent. It is also a featured note in Maison Francis Kirkdjian Aqua Universalis, Hermes Terre d' Hermes, Chanel Bleu de Chanel, Dior Sauvage, Acqua di Parma Colonia, Tom Ford Neroli Portofino, and Giorgio Armani Acqua di Gio Profumo.

Your preferences can guide you in selecting a signature scent that aligns with your taste.

Finding your signature scent is a process that may take time and experimentation. Don't rush the decision; allow yourself opportunity to explore different options and give each fragrance time to develop on your skin before making a final choice.

Ultimately, your signature scent should be one that makes you feel confident, comfortable, and happy. Trust your instincts and choose a fragrance that resonates with you on a personal level.

By exploring different fragrances, considering your preferences, taking your time, testing different fragrances on your skin, and trusting your instincts, you can find a signature scent that reflects your unique personality and style.

pH, Skin Type, and Body Temperature

Choosing the best perfume scent will depend on personal preference and how the fragrance interacts with your unique body chemistry. Test different fragrances on your skin and understand that compounds applied to the skin can be affected by your body chemistry and your environment.

As a result, perfumes can smell differently on different individuals. Skin type, pH levels and body temperature can all affect the absorption level of a fragrance.

It may require some experimentation to find the perfect scent that works well with your skin type, pH levels and body temperature.

If you are having trouble finding your perfect scent, consider learning more about your skin. Scents can smell different on different people depending on whether their skin is more alkaline or acidic.

pH is measured by numbers 0-14. A neutral pH is 7. The lower the number, the more acidic the skin is . . . and the higher the number, the more alkaline. The most ideal pH level for skin is between 4.7 and 5.75.

One of the easiest ways to test the pH of your skin is to use litmus paper. Litmus paper can be purchased at drugstores or online. To conduct the test, simply moisten a piece of litmus paper with distilled water and place it on different areas of your skin, such as the forehead, cheeks, and jawline. The color change on the litmus paper can indicate whether your skin is more acidic (lower pH) or alkaline (higher pH).

Observing the condition of your skin can also provide clues about its pH level. Skin that is more alkaline may be dry, flaky, and prone to irritation, while skin that is more acidic may be oily, acne-prone, or sensitive. Pay attention to how your skin reacts to various skincare products and environmental factors.

If you are unsure about the pH of your skin or if you have specific concerns about your skin condition, it is recommended to consult with a dermatologist. A dermatologist can perform tests to determine your skin's pH level and provide personalized recommendations for skincare products and routines.

Acidic pH Levels

If you have acidic pH levels, it is important to choose a perfume that will work well with your body chemistry and not be altered or affected by the acidity of your skin.

Fragrances that are long-lasting tend to work well with acidic skin as they can withstand the changes in pH throughout the day.

Woody and spicy fragrances often have a strong base note that can help anchor the scent and prevent it from being altered by acidic skin.

Notes such as sandalwood, cedarwood, patchouli, and vetiver can be good choices.

Exotic and amber fragrances are rich and complex, with deep base notes that can complement acidic skin too. These scents often have warmth and depth that can balance out the acidity.

Citrus and floral fragrances, however, may not last as long on your skin.

Test perfume on your skin before purchasing a full bottle. This will allow you to see how the fragrance interacts with your body chemistry and whether it is affected by your acidic pH.

Some popular perfume options that may work well for you include:

- Tom Ford Black Orchid (spicy, floral)

- Chanel Coco Mademoiselle (floral, citrus)

- Yves Saint Laurent Black Opium (sweet, gourmand)

- Guerlain Shalimar (exotic, vanilla)

- Viktor & Rolf Flowerbomb (vanilla, floral)

Alkaline pH Levels

If you have high alkaline pH levels, it is important to explore perfumes that are not altered by the alkalinity of your skin. Fresh and light fragrances are often a good choice as they can help balance out the alkalinity and provide a clean, invigorating scent.

Citrus and green fragrances are refreshing and vibrant, with top notes that can cut through the alkalinity of the skin. Notes such as lemon, bergamot, grapefruit, and green tea can be suitable options.

Floral and fruity fragrances are often soft and delicate, with sweet and uplifting notes that can work well with high alkaline pH. Notes such as rose, jasmine, peach, and raspberry can be good choices too.

Heavy and spicy fragrances may not be the best choice for individuals as these scents can be overpowering and may become too intense on the skin.

Some popular perfume options that may work well for you include:

- Jo Malone London Lime Basil & Mandarin (citrus, aromatic)
- Marc Jacobs Daisy (floral, fruity)
- Dior J'adore (floral, fruity)
- Dolce & Gabbana Light Blue (citrus, aquatic)
- Chanel Chance Eau Tendre (floral, fruity)

Skin Type and Body Temperature

When selecting a fragrance, it's important to consider your skin type. As a general rule, fragrances really pop and last longer when spritzed on oily skin. This is because the natural oils in our skin help to anchor the scent and prevent it from evaporating quickly. On the other hand, if you have dry skin, you may find that fragrances are less intense and do not last as long. In this case, selecting bigger, more powerful scents with staying power is your best bet.

If your skin is neither oily nor dry, you likely have a normal skin type. This is the perfect skin type for fragrances because scents will generally remain true to their composition. This means that the fragrance you smell in the bottle will be the same scent that lingers on your skin throughout the day. With a normal skin type, you have the freedom to experiment with a variety of fragrances and find the perfect one to make your signature scent.

When choosing the perfect scent, it's important to also take into consideration the climate and temperature of your environment. This will ensure that your signature scent not only smells great on you, but also lasts throughout the day, leaving a lasting impression on everyone you encounter.

The climate plays a role in how long your fragrance lasts throughout the day. In colder climates, fragrances tend to linger longer on the skin, giving you a chance to enjoy the scent all day long. On the other hand, in hotter temperatures, fragrances may evaporate quickly, requiring you to reapply throughout the day.

Ultimately, choosing the best perfume will depend on personal preference and how the fragrance interacts with your unique body chemistry and the environment. Your signature scent should not only smell great on your skin, but also complement your environment.

A Caution About Nose Blindness

Over time, our sense of smell can become desensitized to a scent that we are frequently exposed to, making it difficult for us to detect it on ourselves.

"Nose Blindness" refers to the phenomenon where a person becomes accustomed to a particular smell and no longer notices it, even though others may still be able to detect it. This can happen with various scents, including perfumes.

This is why it's important to occasionally switch up perfumes or scents to prevent nose blindness and ensure that we continue to enjoy and benefit from the fragrance. You can also opt for lighter, more subtle scents that are less likely to overwhelm your sense of smell.

If you do experience nose blindness, take a break from using your signature scent every day. Rotate between different scents to prevent your sense of smell from becoming desensitized to the one you love the most.

Elegant Women and Their Signature Scents

Iconic elegant women throughout history have often been associated with signature scents that have become synonymous with their personal style and aura. Some examples of these signature scents include:

Audrey Hepburn – Givenchy L'Interdit: The classic and sophisticated fragrance was created for Audrey Hepburn and has since become synonymous with her timeless elegance and grace.

Grace Kelly – Creed Fleurissimo: This delicate and feminine fragrance was created for Grace Kelly's wedding to Prince Rainier of Monaco and became her signature scent, embodying her regal and refined style.

Jackie Kennedy Onassis – Chanel No. 5: The timeless and iconic fragrance was a favorite of Jackie Kennedy Onassis and perfectly complemented her classic and elegant fashion sense.

Princess Diana – Two perfumes are routinely associated with Princess Diana. Diorissimo by Christian Dior: The fresh and floral fragrance was beloved by Princess Diana and reflected her natural beauty and charm. Bluebell by Floris London: A delicate and floral scent, which perfectly complemented her natural beauty and charm.

Elizabeth Taylor – White Diamonds by Elizabeth Taylor: The luxurious and opulent scent was created by Elizabeth Taylor herself and became her signature fragrance, representing her glamorous and extravagant lifestyle.

These signature scents of iconic elegant women have left a lasting legacy in the world of perfumery, symbolizing their unique personalities and timeless elegance.

My Fragrance Journey

Like most women, I have been drawn to the alluring and enchanting world of fragrances. With each passing day, I find myself enticed by the endless array of scents and the captivating stories they hold.

From the sweet and delicate notes of floral perfumes to the bold and seductive tones of musk, I have explored and indulged in a myriad of fragrances throughout my life. I have always been able to distinguish between a good fragrance and a great one. However, finding a perfume that truly complements my unique style and leaves a lasting impression has been a challenge.

While my pH level runs in a normal range, my fair skin tends to be dry. I live in a desert climate, which is also very dry. As a result, I have tested countless fragrances in search of a rich bold fragrance with plenty of staying power. With each new scent, my hopes would soar, only to be crushed by their fleeting presence or inability to truly encapsulate my essence. But I refused to give up on my mission, determined to discover the fragrance that would truly speak to my soul. And after much trial and error, I finally found my holy grail – the one that would become my signature scent, Delina.

In 2017 Delina was launched as a modern, luxurious, and elegant fragrance from the niche perfume house Parfums de Marly. It is a floral-fruity scent that is known for its sophisticated and feminine aura.

The top notes of Delina include bergamot, lychee, and rhubarb, giving it a fresh and fruity opening.

The heart of Delina is a rich bouquet of Turkish rose, peony, and lily of the valley, adding a floral and romantic touch. The base notes of cashmeran, vanilla, and musk provide a warm and sensual finish to the fragrance.

All Parfum de Marly fragrances have staying power. Delina is no exception. Its longevity and sillage makes it a great choice for me. It is an exceptionally elegant and memorable scent.

Each day as I sit in front of my vanity mirror, I reach for the powder pink tasseled bottle with the chrome and gem top. The moment the fragrance touches my skin, I feel the new day begin. With a light spritz on my wrists and a gentle spray on my neck, I inhale deeply, allowing the familiar aroma to envelop me. Each note tells a story – of evenings in the courtyard, laughter shared with friends, and quiet moments of reflection. This scent is more than just a fragrance; it is an extension of who I am.

I know that how I present myself matters and the fragrance I choose is part of that presentation.

The Invisible Accessory

Imagine the impression your fragrance could leave when you exit a room, a silken trail of scent that continues to enchant long after you have gone. With each step away, the air becomes infused with notes that evoke curiosity and intrigue, inviting those remaining to reminisce about the encounter. Whether it's the warm embrace of vanilla, the crispness of citrus, or the floral bouquet of fresh blooms, your signature scent weaves a story that lingers in the mind, stirring emotions and memories. In that moment, you transform from a mere guest into an unforgettable presence, leaving behind not just an aroma but a captivating essence of who you are.

Your scent, like a lingering memory, leaves a lasting impression that whispers of timeless elegance and understated beauty.

In this moment you know that having a signature scent enhances your personal brand and displays your uniqueness. In this moment you understand the power of a signature scent.

If you have yet to discover your signature scent or if you are interested in uncovering a new personal fragrance, take the time to experiment with different scents. Whether it's a new release from a luxurious brand or a homemade concoction, explore and discover new fragrances. Each perfume is like a little treasure, holding within it the power to evoke memories, emotions, and even transport you to different places and times. And while some may see perfume as a mere accessory, for you, it could become an essential part of your daily routine.

The act of choosing a fragrance in the morning is a ritual that can bring you joy and set the tone for your day. It is a way to express your mood, your personality, and your style without saying a word. So, continue to explore the world of fragrances, seeking out that one scent that will leave a lasting impression and make you feel confident and beautiful.

There is nothing quite as empowering as finding the perfect fragrance that truly captures who you are. Your signature scent can be a powerful tool for self-expression and can add an extra layer of elegance and sophistication to your overall presence and style.

"Living elegantly starts with embracing simplicity."

– Gina Judy

7

THE ELEGANCE OF LIVING

Living elegantly starts with embracing simplicity. Simplicity is not about taking away it is about freeing ourselves. By letting go of excess and concentrating on what is truly important, we can uncover a graceful simplicity that lies at the heart of our being. Embrace the allure of simplicity, not as a limitation, but as a path to a more enriched and satisfying existence.

In a world without the chaos of belongings, constant distractions, and the need to keep up with current fads, envision a life where every decision and interaction is purposeful. This is the true beauty of embracing simplicity in everyday life.

Begin by simplifying your environment, both in the physical world and in your mind. Get rid of unnecessary items, distractions, and anything that is no longer helpful to you. Embrace the concept of minimalism, not as a strict guideline, but as a way of thinking that helps you focus on quality over quantity in all aspects of your life.

Make every moment count by being intentional in your daily routines. Take time to appreciate small things like your morning coffee, a sunny afternoon, or a meaningful conversation with a loved one. These actions, when done with purpose, bring a sense of purpose and meaning to your life, making ordinary moments extraordinary.

Embrace the joy of simplicity in your wardrobe. Discover the elegance of a well-tailored, classic garment, a timeless piece that speaks to your individuality and transcends fleeting trends. Invest in high-quality materials that are meant to last, creating a wardrobe that reflects your values and sense of refinement.

In the realm of dining, simplicity reigns supreme. Embrace the art of mindful eating, savoring each bite and appreciating the flavors and textures of wholesome ingredients. Choose to cook more meals at home, taking the time to create nourishing and delicious dishes that nourish your body and soul.

Embrace the beauty of nature. Take a walk in the park, lose yourself in the serenity of a quiet garden, or simply gaze at the stars on a clear night. Nature's simplicity offers a profound reminder of the elegance that exists in the natural world, inspiring us to live in harmony with our surroundings.

Our intentions go beyond just our things and routines. They affect how we communicate with others. Be mindful when speaking and actively listen and respond thoughtfully. Show the power of sincere compliments by expressing appreciation for the qualities and talents of those around us.

Simple acts of kindness, such as holding a door open for a stranger, offering a helping hand to someone in need, or simply lending a listening ear, create a ripple effect of positivity, spreading elegance and grace throughout the world.

Find elegance in the quiet moments. Seek out solitude, whether it's a few minutes of peaceful meditation or a solitary walk in nature. In the stillness, you can connect with your inner self, cultivate clarity, and discover a sense of peace that transcends the chaos of everyday life.

Finding elegance in the ordinary is not about achieving perfection, but about embracing imperfection with grace. It's about appreciating the beauty of the simple things, the small moments that make up our lives, and the profound connections we share with ourselves, with nature, and with others.

The pursuit of simplicity is not a destination, but a journey. It's a continuous process of letting go, of prioritizing what matters, and of finding joy in the ordinary. By embracing simplicity, we unlock the elegance that lies within us all, creating a life that is both beautiful and meaningful.

Elegance is a State of Mind

Imagine walking through a bustling city, surrounded by a symphony of sights, sounds, and scents. Yet, amidst the chaos, you find yourself fully present, aware of every detail, each sensation a vibrant brushstroke on the canvas of your experience. This is the power of mindfulness – the ability to cultivate a deep sense of presence, to be fully engaged in the here and now, without judgment or distraction.

Mindfulness is not about ignoring the world around you; it's about embracing it with an open and receptive mind. It's about noticing the gentle caress of sunlight on your skin, the soft whisper of wind through leaves, the subtle nuances of a conversation, the intricate dance of emotions that swirl within you. It's about experiencing life with a heightened awareness, appreciating the beauty and complexity of each moment.

Elegance, too, is a state of mind, a way of being. It's about finding grace and harmony in the everyday, in the way we move through the world, in our interactions with others, in the choices we make. And mindfulness becomes the key that unlocks this elegant way of living.

When we cultivate mindfulness, we begin to see the world with a new perspective, a perspective that values depth over superficiality, quality over quantity, presence over distraction. We become more attuned to the subtleties of experience, the nuances of beauty, the power of simple gestures.

Imagine, for instance, a simple act like drinking a cup of tea. Without mindfulness, it's merely a routine, a quick caffeine fix. But with mindfulness, it transforms into an elegant ritual. You find a quiet, sunny spot by a window to set up an elegant tea service with a teapot, teacup, saucer, sugar bowl, creamer, and tray. You select one or two of your favorite teas, using tea bags or loose-leaf tea with a tea infuser. When the water temperature is perfect for the tea you are brewing, you pour it over the leaves or tea bag and allow it to steep for the recommended time. You add a bit of cream and sugar to your taste. You appreciate the warmth of the cup in your hands, the aroma of the leaves, the smooth taste as you savor each sip. It becomes a moment of quiet contemplation, a pause in the whirlwind of daily life.

Mindfulness extends beyond our individual experiences. It also transforms our relationships with others. When we are fully present, we become better listeners, more empathetic, more attuned to the needs and emotions of those around us. We engage in conversations with genuine interest, responding thoughtfully and respectfully.

This mindful approach to communication cultivates a sense of elegance in our interactions. It fosters a deeper understanding, a more authentic connection, a sense of warmth and respect that enriches our lives and the lives of those we touch.

Imagine a business meeting where everyone is fully present, actively listening, engaging in respectful dialogue. The conversation flows effortlessly, ideas are exchanged with clarity and passion, and decisions are made with careful consideration. This is the power of mindfulness applied to the realm of professional interaction, creating a more elegant and productive environment.

Mindfulness also spills over into the way we approach our work, our passions, our creative pursuits. When we are present, we bring a heightened level of focus and intention to our efforts. We become more aware of our strengths and weaknesses, more open to feedback, more willing to experiment and refine our skills. This mindful approach to work cultivates a sense of purpose and excellence, transforming our efforts into something truly elegant.

Think of a master craftsman, meticulously working on a piece of art, each stroke of the brush, each turn of the chisel, guided by a deep sense of presence and intention. They are fully absorbed in the process, their hands moving with grace and precision, their mind focused on creating something beautiful and enduring. This is the elegance of mindfulness applied to the realm of creativity, where passion, precision, and presence converge to create something truly remarkable.

Mindfulness is not a destination; it's a journey, a continuous practice of cultivating awareness and presence. It's about finding beauty in the ordinary, finding meaning in the mundane, finding elegance in every moment of our lives. It's about embracing the world with open arms, with a grateful heart, and a mindful mind.

By cultivating mindfulness, we can unlock a world of elegance, a world where simplicity is valued, presence is cherished, and every experience becomes a source of beauty and fulfillment. It's a journey that starts with a single breath, a single moment, a conscious choice to be fully present in the unfolding drama of life.

Hospitality

Imagine stepping into a home where warmth radiates from every corner. The air is infused with a delicate fragrance, perhaps a hint of lavender or cinnamon, setting the stage for a delightful experience. The furniture is tastefully arranged, inviting you to relax and linger. The conversation flows effortlessly, punctuated by genuine laughter and shared stories. This is the essence of hospitality, an art form that transcends mere obligation and embraces the joy of extending elegance to others.

Hospitality, at its core, is an expression of generosity, a willingness to open your heart and home to those you care about. It's about creating an environment where guests feel truly welcome, valued, and cherished. This doesn't necessarily require grand gestures or extravagant feasts. True hospitality lies in the details, the thoughtful touches that make a difference.

Imagine a beautifully set table, with crisp linens, sparkling glasses, and a centerpiece that reflects the season. The food is prepared with care, highlighting fresh ingredients and flavors that tantalize the palate. Each element, from the carefully chosen tableware to the soft lighting, contributes to an atmosphere that is both inviting and elegant.

But hospitality extends beyond the physical realm. It's about creating a welcoming space for conversation, a safe haven where guests can feel comfortable sharing their thoughts and feelings. It's about active listening, demonstrating genuine interest in their stories, and offering support when needed.

Consider the impact of a sincere compliment, a gesture of kindness, or a thoughtful question. These simple acts of attention can create a sense of connection that deepens the bond between host and guest.

The beauty of hospitality lies in its ability to forge lasting connections. It's about building relationships, creating memories, and nurturing friendships. When you extend hospitality to others, you are not only enriching their lives but also enriching your own.

There's an undeniable elegance to creating a space where people feel seen, heard, and appreciated. It's about fostering a sense of belonging and fostering a shared experience that transcends the ordinary.

As you embark on your journey of cultivating elegance, remember that true refinement extends beyond the superficial. It's about embracing the art of hospitality, creating welcoming environments, and making others feel truly valued. By extending this generosity of spirit, you will not only elevate your own life but also touch the lives of those around you.

To incorporate the elegance of hospitality in your life, begin by setting the stage. Create a welcoming atmosphere in your home. Consider the lighting, the music, and the overall ambiance. A touch of fresh flowers, a warm fireplace, or soft lighting can create a sense of comfort and tranquility.

Embrace simplicity. Don't feel the need to overcomplicate things. A simple, well-prepared meal can be just as enjoyable as a grand feast. Focus on quality ingredients and thoughtful presentation.

Try to engage in meaningful conversations with your guests. Ask them questions about their lives, listen attentively, and share your own stories and experiences.

Go the extra mile. Consider offering small gestures of kindness, such as a warm beverage upon arrival, a thoughtful gift, or a personalized touch. Always express your gratitude to your guests for taking the time to visit. A simple "thank you" can go a long way in creating a sense of appreciation.

Remember, hospitality is a two-way street. Just as it's important to extend warmth and kindness to others, it's equally important to be a gracious guest. Respect your host's time, home, and preferences. Arrive on time, offer to help, and express your appreciation for their generosity.

By embracing the art of hospitality, you can enrich your own life and create a world filled with warmth, connection, and shared experiences. The elegance of living lies not just in the way we present ourselves but also in the way we treat others. Let your home be a sanctuary of hospitality, a place where elegance and connection flourish.

The Elegant Hostess

Whether you are hosting a formal dinner for thirty or a small get together for two, your goal is to greet your guests with an inviting scene as soon as they arrive.

Plan ahead. Make sure to plan out all the details of your event in advance, including the guest list, menu, decorations, special activities, entertainment, favors, and valet or parking. Give yourself plenty of time to arrange catering, entertainment, rental supplies, and secure valet support. Depending on your event, planning ahead could require several weeks or even months lead time.

Plan to create a welcoming atmosphere. Set the mood with soft lighting, music, and pleasant scents to create a warm and inviting environment.

As the hostess, it's important for you to dress appropriately for the occasion. Choose an outfit that is stylish and sophisticated, but also comfortable enough to allow you to move around and interact with your guests. You will be on your feet for the majority of the time, so avoid extremely high heels or shoes that are uncomfortable.

Plan to personally greet your guests. As guests arrive, greet them with a smile and a warm welcome. Offer them a drink or appetizer and help them feel at ease. If you plan on having more than ten guests, consider hiring catering and bar support so you are free to greet and mingle with your guests.

Be a gracious host. Make sure to check in with your guests throughout the event to ensure they are comfortable and having a good time.

Offer to refill their drinks, introduce them to other guests, and make sure they have everything they need.

Make sure to provide a variety of delicious and well-presented food and drinks for your guests to enjoy. Consider incorporating special touches like themed cocktails or a signature dish.

Small details can make a big difference when it comes to hosting a successful event. Pay attention to things like table settings, decorations, music, lighting, and presentation to create a polished and elegant atmosphere. If you are holding an event during the cooler months, consider where guests will hang their coats. If your event is in your home and you have a closet for your own coats, clear your closet ahead of time so guests can hang their coats on nice hangers when they arrive. Avoid having guests pile coats on a bed in a bedroom. Even though most guests are willing to place their coats on a bed in a bedroom, they will appreciate the effort of clearing a closet and providing nice coat hangers that prevent wrinkles and creases.

For larger events, consider hiring a photographer. Professional photographers are adept at capturing candid moments that may go unnoticed by guests. These spontaneous shots often convey the true emotions and atmosphere of the event, creating a more authentic representation of the day. Professional photographs become treasured keepsakes that you can look back on for years to come. They allow you to relive the emotions and experiences of the day, making them invaluable. Sharing photographs with your guests after an event is a lovely way to thank them for coming and it is an opportunity for them to have a lasting memory.

Above all, remember to be gracious, polite, and attentive to your guests' needs. Thank each guest for coming, engage in conversation, and make sure they feel valued and appreciated throughout the event.

When guests leave your event, it's a thoughtful gesture to provide them with a small token of appreciation as a thank-you for attending. Consider giving a personalized favor that reflects the theme of the event, such as a custom candle, with their name or initials on it.

Give guests a mini bottle of wine or champagne which they can enjoy at home as a reminder of the fun they had at your party. Wine and champagne appeals to a broad audience, making it a versatile gift suitable for various types of events. Wine or champagne is associated with celebration and enjoyment. Mini bottles are convenient for guests to take home. They are lightweight and compact, making them easy to carry, unlike larger bottles that may be cumbersome. Mini bottles can also be customized with labels featuring the event name or a personal message. Gifting guests with a mini bottle of wine or champagne is a thoughtful and memorable way to express gratitude, enhance the event experience, and create lasting impressions.

During the holidays, one of my favorite "thank you gifts" to give my guests are mini picture frame ornaments featuring their photograph. Mini frames are a distinctive gift that stands out compared to typical party favors. They also convey effort and creativity that you put thought into the gift. They are lightweight, easy to transport, and can be personalized with names, dates, or themes.

Cover a small holiday tree with mini framed photos of your guests that they can take with them as they leave your event. While this requires a bit of planning ahead of time, your guests will love taking these home and placing them on their own holiday tree. Whether a candid shot from the event or a meaningful image, guests appreciate thoughtful gifts that remind them of their shared experience. A framed photograph can prompt guests to reminisce about the event and the people they shared it with.

Being an elegant hostess also includes the ability to set a beautiful table, as the dining experience is often at the heart of any gathering.

Setting a Beautiful Table

A thoughtfully arranged table not only enhances the aesthetic appeal of the occasion but also sets the tone for conversation, laughter, and, of course, delicious food.

Setting an elegant formal table involves arranging the tableware in an organized manner to create an elegant dining experience.

Start with a clean tablecloth or placemats that do not distract from the tableware or centerpiece. Like a blank canvas, a white linen tablecloth makes a perfect backdrop for any occasion. This will be your base.

Place dinner plates in the center of each setting. Think of each place setting as a little masterpiece in itself, with the dinner plates acting as the focal point.

Put the napkin to the left of the plate or on top of the plate. A special napkin ring or ribbon can add a bit of flair as well as folding the napkin into an interesting design. Pay attention to every detail, ensuring the napkins are folded with precision and any adornments serve to add a touch of sophistication.

The lotus flower fold, for example, can be accomplished in a few easy steps:

- Start with a Flat Napkin – Begin with a square napkin laid flat with the open side facing you.
- Fold in Half – Take the bottom corner and fold it up to meet the top corner to create a triangle.
- Fold Right Corner – Take the right corner and fold it towards the center point, creating a smaller triangle.
- Fold Left Corner – Repeat the previous step with the left corner, folding it towards the center point to create a smaller triangle on the left side.
- Flip Napkin – Carefully flip the napkin over so the folds are now on the bottom and the smooth side is facing up.
- Fold Bottom Point Up –Take the bottom point of the triangle and fold it up towards the top point.
- Starting from the bottom, gently pull up the top layer of the napkin and fold it outward, creating a petal shape. Do this for each layer, pulling up to all four corners to create the petals of the lotus flower.
- Create Petals – Once all layers are pulled up, adjust the petals to make them look full. Place the completed lotus flower napkin on the center of the plate.

A variety of interesting napkin folds can be found with a simple search on Pinterest or YouTube.

Following napkin placement, set the fork to the left of the plate and the knives and spoons to the right. The salad fork should be placed on the outside, followed by the dinner fork, then the knives (blade facing the plate) and spoons.

Place the water glass above the knives on the right side. Glassware should be clean, free of spots and ready to be filled. Add any additional glassware or stemware to the right, above the water glass. An easy way to remember what side to place the drinks is to make a lower case "d" with your right hand.

Place the bread plate above the forks on the left side. An easy way to remember what side to place the bread is to make a lower case "b" with your left hand.

Add a dessert spoon and fork above the plate horizontally or diagonally.

Consider adding a decorative centerpiece or candles to enhance the table setting.

Soft candlelight is ideal for the evening meal as it gently illuminates and elevates the table.

These are just general guidelines. Table settings can vary depending on the formality of the occasion and personal preferences.

To expand your table setting knowledge and other entertainment tips, explore articles, blogs, and social media platforms like Instagram.

Host Gift Etiquette

In many cultures, bringing a gift for the host is a common social norm that reflects good manners and etiquette.

A host puts time, effort, and resources into organizing a gathering. Bringing a gift for the host when attending is a thoughtful gesture that shows appreciation and gratitude. A thoughtful gift can also set a positive tone for the gathering and contribute to a warm and friendly atmosphere, making the host feel appreciated and encouraging a sense of community among guests.

The gift doesn't have to be extravagant or expensive. It can be something simple like a small bouquet of flowers, a bottle of wine, or a decorative candle. Take the time to choose the gift with care to convey thoughtfulness and consideration. Think about the host's interests and preferences. I am a fan of adding a crystal wine stopper with a bottle of wine or a set of monogram napkins with a basket of cookies.

I cannot think of a situation where I would include "gifts are welcome" or "no gifts please" on an invitation so hopefully you do not run into this situation often. However, there may be unusual situations when you receive a birthday or holiday invitation that indicates "no gifts please". In those situations, try to respect the host's request regarding a wrapped gift. If you are a big gift giver, like I am, feel free to bring a bottle of wine or a small candle to the host with a note thanking them for the invitation.

Social Media

Leveraging social media can allow you to expand your knowledge by providing access to a wealth of ideas and expert tips that can inspire and enhance your skills. So, while social media is not all together a bad thing, it does bring a certain set of risks that require strategies to manage with poise and grace.

First and foremost, remember that what you put on social media eternally remains on the internet. What is shared online can have lasting effects on a person's reputation. Posts that may seem harmless at the moment can be misinterpreted, taken out of context, or come back to haunt someone in the future, especially in professional settings.

Be mindful of what you post and do not overshare. Just as an elegant woman does not publicly share a lot of personal information, an elegant woman limits personal information shared on social media. This is for safety reasons as well as protection related to your personal brand. Remember, your personal brand is how you are viewed and remembered. It is how you promote yourself and how others perceive you, both online and offline.

Sharing personal information on social media can expose individuals to privacy risks. Personal details about one's life relationships, or finances can be misused by others, leading to identity theft, scams, or harassment.

Don't tag people in photos without asking their permission. We each have our own personal brand, and we change over time. For this reason, it is not appropriate to post old photographs from high school or college days.

Do not discuss or disclose private matters, particularly personal problems, conflicts, or issues, in public or to others outside of the immediate situation. Don't share disputes, relationship troubles, or other personal issues on social media. Publicly airing personal issues or conflicts can invite unwanted opinions, judgments, or criticism from others.

An elegant woman might choose to post photos and comments on social media, but how she does so can reflect her sense of style, confidence, and personal brand. As elegance is often associated with qualities like grace, poise, and sophistication, it is important that posts on social media reflect grace, poise, and sophistication.

If she shares photos to inspire, connect, or express herself, it can be seen as an elegant use of the platform. The intention behind the post often matters more than the act of posting itself.

Elegant women value their time and energy, and therefore, they limit their use of social media. Instead of wasting hours scrolling through endless feeds, they prioritize activities that bring value to their lives. This includes reading, learning new things, working on personal projects, and engaging in activities that enrich their lives and the lives of others.

Elegant women understand the importance of social interaction, but they do not let it consume their lives. Social media can be a great tool for connecting with others and staying up-to-date with current events. However, elegant women recognize the negative impact it can have on their mental well-being. They understand that social media can often lead to feelings of inadequacy and comparison, which can lower their self-esteem. Therefore, they choose to limit their time on these platforms and instead, focus on activities that promote growth and positivity.

Social media serves as a platform where users can find inspiration, access educational content, and build connections with others. It is not a place for negativity or unkindness. It is perfectly okay to unfollow or block someone that is posting things that are inappropriate or make you feel uncomfortable.

In today's digital age, it is easy to get caught up in the world of social media. However, elegant women understand the importance of maintaining a balance between social media and real-life experiences. They prioritize their time and energy towards activities that align with their values and personal preferences, rather than mindlessly scrolling through endless feeds. By limiting their time on social media, elegant women are able to maintain a healthy and fulfilling lifestyle.

Text Messaging

Where social media tends to be viewed by the general public, text messages are usually private and not visible to the general public. But like social media, text messaging generates risks that also require skill to manage with elegance.

Text messaging often allows for real-time communication, enabling immediate responses. Messaging in this format is primarily text-based, although messaging can include images, videos, and voice messages. The format is straightforward and focused on direct dialogue.

Texting elegantly involves communicating with clarity, respect, and a touch of grace. In this spirit, avoid excessive abbreviations and slang. Use complete sentences, appropriate punctuation, and correct spelling to convey sophistication and care in your communication.

As text lacks the nuances of voice and facial expressions, be mindful of your tone – and the perception of your tone. Do not use all capital letters as it can come across as shouting. Choose your words carefully to express your thoughts clearly and respectfully. Avoid casual language that may come off as too informal or dismissive.

Be mindful of when you send your texts. Unless it is urgent, do not send messages late at night or during times when the recipient might be busy.

Always use polite language and consider adding a friendly touch with an emoji, but do not overuse emojis as it can detract from the elegance of your text.

Finally, avoid the use of coarse language. Coarse language can be offensive and may alienate individuals. It can harm your brand's image, undermine your credibility, and negatively affect how others perceive you. Always use respectful language that fosters a positive atmosphere and reflects a positive image.

Traveling

Traveling with elegance involves a combination of style, grace, and practicality. Just as in the day-to-day style of an elegant woman, incorporate classic, tailored silhouettes in your travel outfits. While comfort is important, aim for a sophisticated and polished look. Choose stylish clothing that reflects your sense of elegance, considering both the destination and mode of travel.

Select timeless clothing items such as a well-fitted blazer, tailored trousers, a little black dress, and a classic trench coat. These can be mixed and matched for various occasions.

Favor neutrals and classic colors like gray, navy, and black for a timeless and polished look. Footwear should reflect elegance as well as comfort. Select a lower heel or a flat shoe, but ensure footwear remains stylish. Low heeled pumps or classic ballet flats ensure you walk with ease and remain graceful. Depending on the destination, a simple pair of classic white tennis shoes can be worn with tailored shorts, a structured mini dress, or fitted pair of jeans.

Folding travel flats are fabulous for those extended travel times that might require wearing heels for departure and arrival. Changing to flats will significantly improve your comfort level during a long flight, especially considering feet can swell while flying. Tieks travel flats by Gavrieli are an example of a versatile travel flat that is durable, stylish, and foldable. They come in a variety of colors and fold into a small space that can easily be tucked in a side pocket of a carryon tote or train case.

If boating, remember to bring a pair of deck shoes in a stylish tote. Do not wear your deck shoes except on the boat. Deck shoes are designed with non-marking rubber soles to prevent scuffing and damaging the boat's deck. Wearing them only on the boat ensures that the soles remain clean and effective. By wearing deck shoes only while on the boat, you help ensure safety, cleanliness, and longevity for the shoes and the vessel itself. When it comes to deck shoes, comfort, grip, and water resistance are essential features. Sperry's Top-Sider "Authentic Original" model is particularly stylish, popular, and recommended.

Incorporate a silk scarf for a touch of sophistication. A 90 cm (35 inch) square silk scarf, for example, can be worn around your neck, in your hair, or tied to your bag.

A good pair of oversized or chic sunglasses for sun protection and a touch of glamour is a must.

Embrace a minimal aesthetic and focus on clean lines and simple designs for an understated elegance over ostentation. Pack versatile pieces that can be dressed up or down. Bring only what you need to avoid excessive baggage. A well-planned capsule wardrobe can help you look chic without overpacking.

Try using a modified version of the 3 – 3 – 3 rule to design a travel wardrobe capsule that offers a dozen or more ensemble choices. The concept involves selecting nine pieces of clothing, broken down into three categories: 3 tops, 3 bottoms, and 3 outer layers.

- Three tops: A combination of short sleeved, long sleeved, and sleeveless tops.
- Three Bottoms: A mix of pants, shorts, and skirts.
- Three Outer Layers: Choices include blazers, sweaters, or jackets.

To ensure an elegant and impeccable style it is usually necessary to modify the rule to include additional pieces such as swimwear, evening wear, and ensembles for special activities.

Experiment with packing cubes and dust bags to keep your luggage organized and neat. I am a fan of using tissue paper to ensure my clothes remain wrinkle-free and in pristine condition upon arrival at my destination.

Choose a hairstyle that is easy to manage but still looks polished. Loose waves, a sleek ponytail, or a classic bun can all convey elegance.

An Elegant Woman's Luggage

When looking for elegant luggage, it's important to consider both style and functionality.

Whether you prefer a soft or hard side option, select luggage that reflects your personal preferences and needs. Stackable luggage offers several advantages, making it a practical and efficient choice for packing and transport. Depending on the destination and mode of travel, stacking smaller bags on top of larger ones makes it easier to maneuver through airports and train stations.

While there are a number of excellent luggage lines, Tumi is known for its high-quality, durable luggage with a sleek and professional design. When flying commercially or traveling with multiple transfers, Tumi's patented TUMI Tracer for lost luggage recovery is a value-add feature worthy of consideration. Other brands to explore include Samsonite Black Label, Away, Rimowa, Louis Vuitton, and Prada.

A makeup travel or train case is a stylish and practical way to organize hygiene and makeup essentials while traveling. While you want to keep your makeup simple and fresh when traveling, you will also want to be prepared to ensure an elegant journey. In addition to a simplified makeup kit, a well-planned train case will include cleanser, sunscreen, serum, moisturizer, makeup remover, setting spray, eye drops, perfume, body wash, deodorant, medications, and other essentials.

Even if you plan to have professional blowouts during your travels, it's wise to include travel-sized shampoo, conditioner, styling products, and a small hairbrush or comb. Include a few hair ties, bobby pins, a headband or clip. Even if you have your nails professionally manicured, include a small nail file, nail clippers, and travel size nail polish or topcoat. As a fan of the French manicure, I tend to include a French Manicure White Tip Pen by Sally Hansen for emergency touch ups.

If you love hats, like I do, consider investing in a small to medium size hatbox piece of luggage to prevent damage during travel. Hatboxes are a standout feature with a nostalgic quality, reminiscent of a bygone era when travel was often more glamorous. Carrying a hatbox exudes a sense of style and evokes an image of classic Hollywood.

Beyond carrying hats, a hatbox can double as a chic storage solution for other items, such as scarves or smaller accessories, combining practicality with elegance. Carrying a hatbox also suggests that you take pride in your appearance and are willing to invest in fashionable pieces, projecting an image of sophistication and thoughtfulness in your travel style.

As a fan of the beret, a smaller size hatbox usually meets my needs, but a larger brim boater hat may require a medium size hat carrier to maintain its shape. Calpak is one of my favorite brands as it is known for its stylish and functional hatboxes. The "Ambeur" Collection includes a hatbox that is lightweight, making it easy to carry and maneuver.

Embrace Graceful Travel Etiquette

Practicing graceful travel etiquette enhances your travel experience and positively impacts those around you. Give yourself plenty of time to check in, go through security, and board your transportation. Being on time shows respect for others' schedules.

When interacting with airline employees and fellow travelers, greet them with a smile and a friendly "hello". Use "please" and "thank you" to express gratitude. Keep your voice low when talking on the phone or with companions, as loud conversations can be disruptive to others.

When seated, be mindful of the space around you. Avoid encroaching on others' space, especially in confined areas like airplanes and trains. If you must reach across someone (e.g., for your bag), ask politely first rather than assuming it's okay. If listening to music or watching videos, use headphones to avoid disturbing those around you.

Whether in a hotel room, airport lounge, or train carriage, always tidy up after yourself. Dispose of trash properly and leave communal areas as you find them.

Tip housekeeping and butler staff to express gratitude for their hard work and care that goes into maintaining your room and assisting with your needs. Tipping is a small gesture of appreciation that can go a long way. Tipping is not only a way to show your appreciation, but it can encourage staff to maintain high standards of service. When these hard-working individuals know that their efforts might be rewarded, they are often more motivated to go above and beyond for their guests.

Cash is often the preferred method for tipping as it allows the staff to keep the tip directly. To add a personal touch, leave the tip in an envelope with a thank-you note to express your appreciation for their service.

Check with your hospitality experts regarding the tipping amount but tip according to the number of nights you are staying. For example, $5-$10 per night for housekeeping and varying amounts for butlers based on the level of service. Depending on the level of luxury and the extent of service provided, it is common to tip butlers between

$20-$50 per day. If the butler goes above and beyond or provides personalized services (like organizing special events, making reservations, or handling special requests), you may want to tip $50 – $100 or more to reflect the level of service.

If you are staying for an extended period, consider tipping at the end of the stay rather than daily. A total of 10%-20% of the total cost of butler service is a reasonable guideline for longer stays.

Travel can sometimes be unpredictable. Maintain a calm demeanor, especially during delays or inconveniences, and show understanding toward staff and fellow travelers. If plans change, embrace the situation gracefully and be open to alternative arrangements.

The Inelegant Traveler

An inelegant traveler is the opposite of an "elegant" traveler. This individual lacks grace, refinement, and sophistication while traveling.

This is the traveler that emerges from a crowded boarding area, struggling with an overstuffed duffel bag, wearing house slippers, flannel pajama pants, and giving off an air of neglect rather than casual comfort.

This is the traveler that is difficult to not notice because their voice carries across the terminal. As they fish for their travel documents, it is clear that elegance has been left behind, replaced instead by a chaotic spirit regarding the journey.

An inelegant traveler exhibits an unstylish presence that often reflects a lack of attention to aesthetics, coordination, or appropriateness for the travel situation. Wearing flip-flops, worn-out sneakers, clunky shoes, or uncomfortable shoes for walking or standing for a long period are not suitable for travel.

Wearing clothes that are too tight or too loose also presents an unflattering appearance.

Poorly coordinated outfits appear chaotic and unrefined. This may involve random combinations of clothing that lack cohesion or thought, such as pajama pants with a dressy top. This may also involve clashing colors and patterns that don't complement each other.

Wearing clothing or accessories that are overly branded or logo-heavy, can come off as tacky rather than stylish.

Wearing items that are too casual or sloppy, such as sweatpants, oversized t-shirts, or overly baggy clothing that lacks structure fails to present an elegant image. Neglecting to dress appropriately for the destination or occasion (e.g., wearing beachwear in a city), also fails to present an elegant image.

Avoid overloading on accessories that clutter the look, such as multiple chunky jewelry pieces or scarves that don't match the outfit. This includes carrying oversized bags or backpacks that are impractical and unflattering.

Unkept hair or a lack of basic hygiene practices, such as not refreshing makeup or skincare during travel, is also indicative of a lack of elegance.

Instead of traveling in a chaotic, haphazard fashion, strive to travel with more style and grace. Striving to be an elegant traveler is not just about appearances, it's about cultivating a mindset that values respect, mindfulness, and appreciation for the diverse world we explore.

By embodying elegance, you set a standard for yourself and others. Your demeanor can inspire fellow travelers to adopt a more respectful and thoughtful approach, creating a more pleasant environment for everyone.

An elegant traveler enhances not only their own experience but the experiences of those around them.

Gratitude

Gratitude, that simple yet profound act of acknowledging the good in our lives, is more than just a polite gesture. It is a powerful force that has the ability to transform our outlook, enhance our well-being, and cultivate a more elegant approach to life. The cultivation of gratitude is a journey of self-discovery, leading us to appreciate the often-overlooked beauty and richness that surrounds us.

Imagine, for a moment, the world through the eyes of someone who practices gratitude. Instead of fixating on what is lacking, they focus on what is present. A beautiful sunrise, a heartfelt conversation with a loved one, a quiet moment of reflection in nature – these are the moments that spark joy and contentment. In this state of appreciation, we find ourselves more resilient in the face of adversity, better equipped to navigate life's inevitable challenges with grace and poise.

The benefits of gratitude extend far beyond personal fulfillment. It creates a ripple effect, positively impacting those around us. When we express gratitude to others, we acknowledge their contributions, strengthening our bonds and fostering a sense of connection. We create a more positive and harmonious environment, where kindness and respect prevail.

Cultivating gratitude isn't about ignoring the realities of life or pretending everything is perfect. It's about making a conscious effort to shift our perspective, to appreciate the little things that often go unnoticed. It's about finding beauty in the mundane, in the simple act of breathing fresh air or enjoying a cup of coffee in the morning.

To cultivate gratitude in your daily life, begin by keeping a gratitude journal. Take a few minutes each day to write down things you are grateful for, big or small. This simple act of reflection can help you shift your focus to the positive aspects of your life. In addition, practice mindful appreciation. Engage in activities with a conscious intention to appreciate them. Whether it's savoring a meal, listening to music, or enjoying a walk in nature, immerse yourself fully in the experience and notice the details that bring you joy.

Take the time to thank those who have made a positive impact on your life. A heartfelt thank you note, a sincere compliment, or a simple gesture of kindness can go a long way in strengthening relationships and fostering a sense of appreciation.

Expressing gratitude and showing appreciation are not only polite gestures, but also a reflection of one's upbringing and character. It demonstrates a level of refinement and civility, displaying a person's good breeding and grace. A simple "thank you" can go a long way in making someone feel valued and acknowledged. It shows that you have taken the time to recognize their efforts and that you are grateful for their presence in your life.

In a society where self-centeredness and entitlement are prevalent, expressing gratitude is a breath of fresh air and sets individuals apart. It also fosters positive relationships, as people are more likely to reciprocate kindness and generosity when they feel appreciated. Moreover, showing gratitude can improve one's own well-being, as it promotes positive emotions and reduces feelings of resentment or entitlement. So, the next time someone does something kind for you remember to say, "thank you" and spread the message of kindness.

To develop the art of sending thank you notes, identify an area of your home where you keep high-quality stationery, writing pens, seals for envelopes, and stamps. This will make it convenient for you to take a few minutes and prepare a note of thanks.

In my home I have stocked my private office with luxurious stationery, stamps for mailing, and gorgeous ink pens. To encourage writing I maintain a neat and inviting desk decorated with beautiful flowers, glamorous accents, and a sleek white writing chair. I understand that if I make my work area inviting, I will enjoy spending time there. If I spend more time in my office, I am more likely to take the time to send a "thank you" note or make the necessary arrangements to ensure a lovely bouquet of flowers arrives unexpectedly for someone that has shown me lovely kindness.

Cultivating gratitude is not a one-time event; it is an ongoing journey of conscious awareness and intentional practice. As you incorporate these practices into your life, you will gradually shift your perspective, embracing the abundance that surrounds you. You will find yourself more resilient, more joyful, and more connected to the beauty of life.

For a life of elegance, take the time to develop the art of gratitude. Development of these skills will allow you to appreciate the small moments, the simple joys, and the extraordinary beauty that exists all around you. It is a reminder that even in the midst of life's challenges, there is always something to be grateful for. By cultivating a spirit of gratitude, you cultivate a more elegant and fulfilling life.

Kindness

The essence of kindness is a graceful dance, a symphony of compassion and generosity that resonates through the hearts and minds of those around us. It is not merely a fleeting gesture but a profound philosophy of living that transforms the world into a more beautiful and harmonious place.

Imagine walking down a bustling city street, the air thick with the hum of activity. In the midst of this urban tapestry, a single act of kindness can illuminate the path like a beacon of hope. A warm smile exchanged with a stranger, a helping hand offered to someone struggling with a heavy bag, a simple word of encouragement to a weary soul. These seemingly insignificant acts have the power to ripple outward, creating a chain reaction of positive energy that touches countless lives.

Kindness is not confined to grand gestures or extravagant displays of generosity. It flourishes in the quiet moments, in the small acts of consideration that enrich our daily interactions. A handwritten note of gratitude, a thoughtful gesture of support, a listening ear offered to a friend in need – these are the building blocks of an elegant life, woven together by threads of compassion and understanding.

There is true elegance in kindness. Elegance lies in the ability to uplift and inspire.

Your kindness is a potent antidote to the negativity and cynicism that can pervade your world. It is a reminder of the inherent goodness that resides within us, a spark of light that ignites compassion within the heart. When you choose kindness as your guiding principle, you unlock the potential for a more harmonious and fulfilling life.

Kindness is not merely a social virtue but a spiritual practice. It is a way of cultivating inner peace and harmony, a path to self-discovery and enlightenment. When you extend kindness to others, you cultivate a sense of connection and unity, as we are all interconnected.

Remember, kindness is not a destination but a journey. It is a lifelong commitment to making the world a better place, one act of kindness at a time. It is a path that leads us towards a more refined and fulfilling life, a world where kindness is not a luxury but a necessity, where the beauty of humanity shines brightest.

"True elegance isn't about achieving a rigid standard, but about discovering what brings harmony and joy to our lives."
– Gina Judy

8

CULTIVATING AN ELEGANT LIFESTYLE

Our daily rhythm, like a well-conducted orchestra, sets the tone for our lives. In a fast-paced world full of distractions, creating a routine that promotes elegance is more than just superficial; it's a meaningful way to take care of ourselves, live mindfully, and find inner harmony. This rhythm doesn't mean strict schedules or suffocating limits, but rather a deliberate structure that helps us infuse grace, mindfulness, and purpose into our daily activities.

Picture a day that flows with purpose and calm, where every moment is a calculated stride towards a more refined life. This graceful routine isn't about reaching flawlessness, but about crafting a peaceful haven amidst the commotion of daily life. It begins with awakening the mind and body with mindful intent. This could be a quiet moment of reflection while sipping tea, a gentle yoga session, or a brief stroll in nature, allowing the mind to quiet and the body to awaken with purpose.

Start the day with mindfulness to set the tone and stay present while completing tasks. Throughout the day, take short moments for self-care. A quick five-minute meditation during work can help refocus and restore clarity. Enjoy a nourishing lunch by savoring the flavors and textures of your food instead of rushing. End the day with a peaceful routine, like reading, listening to calming music, or reflecting before bedtime.

This structure helps us find order and balance in life, making it easier to handle challenges. It encourages us to focus on our health and inner peace. By following a routine that aligns with our values and goals, we create room for personal growth and becoming our best selves.

This daily rhythm brings tranquility and focus, leading to a sense of purpose and achievement. By living intentionally, we gain a greater sense of control and ownership over our lives. This purpose-driven mindset not only affects our personal lives, but also impacts our interactions with others and the world. It promotes generosity, mindfulness, and a desire to make a positive impact in our communities.

Remember, true elegance isn't about achieving a rigid standard, but about discovering what brings harmony and joy to our lives. It's about creating a framework that supports our growth, nourishes our spirit, and allows us to move through the world with grace and intention. The journey of cultivating an elegant lifestyle is a personal one, a journey of self-discovery and refinement. It's about finding the rituals and routines that resonate with our individual aspirations, helping us to live with intention, grace, and a sense of true elegance.

This daily rhythm of mindfulness goes beyond our personal well-being and influences all aspects of our lives. It encourages us to prioritize quality over quantity, emphasizing the importance of longevity and sustainability. By choosing well-made and intentional items, we establish a harmonious and sustainable relationship with our belongings and the world around us.

This mindful mindset also extends to our living spaces. Creating an elegant home is not about following trends or accumulating possessions, but about creating a peaceful and inspiring environment that reflects our unique style. We can achieve this by selecting furniture and decor that aligns with our aesthetic preferences, creating a space that is both visually appealing and functional. Simplifying and decluttering our homes and lives also allows for clarity and intention to thrive.

Elegance and intentionality can transcend our interactions with the world. When we travel, we carry this mindful approach with us, treating others with respect and embracing new cultures with an open mind. By choosing experiences that align with our values, travel becomes more than just a vacation, but a journey of self-discovery and personal growth.

The ability to find elegance in unexpected situations, navigating challenges with grace and resilience, is a testament to the power of a mindful approach. When life throws us curveballs, we can draw upon the inner strength and composure we've cultivated through our daily routines to meet these challenges with grace and a positive attitude.

The journey towards an elegant lifestyle is not about being perfect, but about continuously evolving and improving. It's about finding what inspires us and enjoying the process of self-discovery. Elegance is not a goal, but a way of living that involves grace, mindfulness, and purpose. By weaving these elements into our daily lives, we not only change ourselves, but also add to the beauty and balance of our surroundings.

In today's society where trends and possessions are constantly changing, there is grace in thinking carefully about your purchasing choices. This practice is referred to as "mindful consumption".

Mindful consumption promotes an elegant and responsible lifestyle by encouraging individuals to carefully choose and invest in high-quality items. Rather than accumulating excessive possessions, mindful consumption focuses on curating a collection of timeless and durable pieces. It values craftsmanship and longevity over fleeting trends.

Mindful consumption is not solely about buying expensive objects, but rather making conscious choices and understanding the true value of an item. This involves researching materials, appreciating craftsmanship, and considering the impact of our purchases. By prioritizing quality over quantity, we actively act with elegance and contribute to a more sustainable future. Choosing quality over quantity allows us to cultivate elegance through a more thoughtful and curated approach to our belongings.

Quality Over Quantity

Invest in Timeless Pieces

Instead of chasing every fleeting trend, focus on building a wardrobe filled with classic items that transcend seasons and years. A well-tailored blazer, a little black dress, a pair of quality leather boots – these are the pieces that will remain stylish for years to come.

Choose Durable Materials

Look for items crafted from high-quality materials like natural fibers (cotton, linen, silk) and durable leathers, ensuring they withstand the test of time and multiple wearings.

Prioritize Craftsmanship

Appreciation for craftsmanship is a cornerstone of mindful consumption. Seek out items made by artisans, brands known for their meticulous attention to detail, and quality control. These pieces will not only be more durable but also tell a story of dedication and skill.

Shop Less, Buy Better

Shopping less and buying better is a sustainable and mindful approach to consumerism that can lead to a more intentional lifestyle and a positive impact on the environment. Consider if an item is essential or just a want. Ask yourself if you can live without it for a while.

Look for well-made products that will last longer. Higher quality items often save you money overall. Rather than impulsively buying numerous items, invest in fewer pieces of higher quality. This allows for a more curated wardrobe and a more conscious approach to your purchases.

Appreciating Longevity

The Joy of Repair

Embrace the art of repair and restoration. Instead of discarding an item with a small tear or a loose button, take the time to mend it. This not only extends the life of the garment but also fosters a connection with your belongings.

Caring for Your Possessions

Treat your belongings with care. Properly store and maintain your clothing, shoes, and accessories, ensuring they remain in excellent condition. This demonstrates respect for their quality and longevity.

Cultivating a Sense of Value

Appreciate the Story

Consider the journey behind each item you own. Where was it made? Who crafted it? What materials were used? Understanding the history of your possessions adds a layer of depth and appreciation.

Create a Capsule Wardrobe

Build a curated wardrobe filled with versatile pieces that can be easily mixed and matched, creating a sense of harmony and elegance in your daily style.

The Joy of Simplicity

Embrace the elegance of simplicity. Choose items with clean lines, classic silhouettes, and minimal embellishments. This approach to fashion emphasizes quality and timeless appeal.

Mindful consumption involves making conscious and thoughtful decisions. It involves a change in mindset, prioritizing quality over quantity, and committing to sustainability. By adopting this approach, we can build a more elegant and sustainable future, one step at a time. It's not about giving up things we enjoy, but rather appreciating their true worth, fostering elegance, and leading a mindful and sustainable lifestyle.

Symphony of Personal Style

Your home reflects your inner self, a haven where you can relax, recharge, and express your unique style. Cultivating a sophisticated home is not about rigid guidelines or conforming to a particular aesthetic, but rather about creating a space that resonates with your being and evokes a sense of tranquility, ingenuity, and refined living.

Think of your home as a blank canvas on which you can manifest your individual style. Each element, from the furnishings to the artwork, should contribute to a cohesive narrative that reflects your taste and persona. Embrace the art of selection, choosing pieces that speak to you, whether it be the timeless charm of a traditional armchair, the vibrant liveliness of a colorful tapestry, or the serene beauty of a minimalist sculpture. Your home should serve as a testament to your passions, interests, and the stories you wish to tell.

A Tidy, Clutter Free Environment

A 2009 study conducted by researchers at UCLA's Center on Everyday Lives and Families examined the relationship between home environments, stress levels, and family dynamics. Researchers noted that clutter created a sense of chaos and overwhelm, leading to increased cortisol levels – the hormone associated with stress. The study highlighted the importance of a tidy, organized home for mental well-being.

An organized home free of clutter minimizes cleaning time and offers the opportunity to relax without the mental to-do list that can nag at you.

To minimize clutter and create a stress-free environment, embrace an organized and minimalist mindset. Consider designating specific areas in your home as clutter-free zones to encourage organization and tidiness. Invest in storage solutions (bins, shelves, organizers) that fit your space and lifestyle. Get rid of damaged shoes, shoes that hurt, stretched out underwear, clothes that cannot be repaired, things you don't love, and anything that you won't wear.

Make sure everything has a designated spot. Once there is a place for everything, develop the habit of putting things away instead of putting things down.

Focus on maintaining a home that works for you, not against you.

A Haven for Relaxation

An elegant home is a sanctuary, a haven where you can escape the demands of the outside world and find solace. Invest in comfortable furniture, soft textures, and soothing colors that promote relaxation and tranquility. The gentle glow of candlelight, the soft melody of classical music, or the aroma of essential oils can further enhance the sense of serenity. This sanctuary should be your personal oasis, where you can decompress, reflect, and reconnect with yourself.

A Catalyst for Creativity

An elegant home should inspire creativity and spark new ideas. This doesn't necessarily mean a studio filled with artistic supplies; it's more about fostering an environment that encourages contemplation and self-expression. Ample natural light, an inspiring view, or even a dedicated corner for quiet reflection can stimulate the imagination.

Imagine a spacious room with an abundance of natural light flooding through floor-to-ceiling windows, offering a panoramic view of the cityscape. The soft, neutral tones of the walls create a calm atmosphere, while the sleek, minimalist furniture adds a touch of contemporary sophistication.

Let your desk take center stage and adorn it with a carefully curated selection of accessories, including a sleek laptop, a delicate glass pen holder, or a small crystal vase of flowers. A carefully selected photo frame with a favorite quote or perhaps a photo of a loved one is a lovely touch for your desktop.

Include a beautifully upholstered chair in a soft neutral leather that provides both comfort and style, ensuring productivity throughout those long work hours. On surrounding shelves, display a few carefully selected books that offer a glimpse into your diverse interests and intellectual pursuits.

An elegant, modern office or workspace should be an extension of your refined taste and a testament to your pursuit of excellence.

The Art of Minimalism

While embracing personal style is crucial, there's a certain elegance in simplicity. The art of minimalism doesn't necessarily mean living with bare walls and sparse furnishings; it's about creating a space that feels intentional and uncluttered.

A minimal design emphasizes simplicity and clarity. When you strip away unnecessary elements, the focus is placed on what truly matters – the design is then more accessible and easier to understand.

Every object should have a purpose and contribute to a sense of harmony. Not only is a minimal environment pleasing, but it is also practical and efficient.

Minimalism conveys a luxurious feel and has a timeless quality.

Creating a Sanctuary

Consider incorporating the following elements to create a home that radiates elegance:

A Neutral Color Palette

Choose a color scheme that evokes a sense of calm and sophistication. Neutrals like creams, grays, and blues can create a timeless backdrop, while pops of color can add accents of personality.

Lighting

Natural light is a beautiful source of elegance but consider strategically placed lamps and dimmers to create a soft, inviting ambiance.

Consider maximizing light with large windows or using soft lighting to create a cozy atmosphere.

Scent

Subtle fragrances like lavender, vanilla, or citrus can enhance the sense of relaxation and create a welcoming atmosphere.

Sound

Create a serene soundscape by playing calming music, nature sounds, or the gentle hum of a water fountain.

Creating a Sense of Place

Beyond the physical elements, cultivating an elegant home involves creating a sense of place. This goes beyond aesthetics; it's about imbuing your space with memories, experiences, and a sense of belonging.

Design areas in your home that cater to specific activities or functions, such as a reading nook, an art studio, an office area, or a meditation space. This not only enhances usability but also gives each area a distinct character.

Bringing nature indoors through houseplants or natural elements can create a calming environment and connect you to the outdoors.

Define different areas in an open space through furniture arrangement or rugs. This helps to create distinct atmospheres for various activities, making the home feel more cohesive and intentional.

Display cherished objects, photographs, and art that evoke meaningful moments and create a sense of connection to the past.

Make your home a comfortable retreat. Use textiles like cushions and throws to create a warm, inviting atmosphere. Comfort can enhance the emotional connection to a space.

Ensure the smell of your home involves a combination of cleanliness, proper ventilation, and the use of pleasant scents. Allow fresh air to circulate by opening windows whenever possible. This helps remove stale air and bring in pleasant outdoor scents.

Keep bathrooms clean and well-ventilated. Regularly clean kitchen appliances, including refrigerator, oven, dishwasher, and garbage disposal. Regularly dust and remove dirt and allergens that can cause unpleasant odors. Clean linens, curtains, and upholstery periodically. Fabrics can absorb odors over time, so washing them can help keep your home smelling fresh.

Remember, elegance is a journey, not a destination.

Cultivating an elegant home is an ongoing process of refinement and expression. As your tastes evolve, so will your home. Approach it with intention, a touch of whimsy, and a commitment to creating a space that reflects your inner world and inspires a life of grace and sophistication.

Travel

Traveling offers the chance to enrich our lives and embrace elegance outside of our everyday routines. It goes beyond looks and involves behaving respectfully, adjusting to new settings with grace, and approaching new experiences with an open mind.

Picture yourself arriving in a foreign city, surrounded by the sights and sounds of a vibrant new culture. The busy airport and fast-moving crowds may feel chaotic, but there is still room for grace. Elegance in travel is not about fitting into strict norms, but rather cherishing the adventure with awareness and appreciation for the diverse cultures you encounter.

Choose comfortable yet stylish clothing for long trips, such as breathable fabrics that resist wrinkles and stretching. Pick neutral colors that complement you and match the places you'll be visiting.

When packing, choosing high-quality clothing can enhance your travel experience by ensuring comfort, durability, and style.

Whether traveling within the states or internationally, take time to plan your clothing carefully. The following is a list of some of my favorites for traveling abroad:

- A versatile tailored double-breasted blazer in white, navy, or black
- A wrinkle-resistant black or white wrap-dress
- Black fitted ankle length pants
- High quality tailored pants
- High-quality jeans in white or medium blue
- Tailored shorts in white or a neutral color
- A wrinkle resistant form fitting or compression top

- A silk blouse in a neutral color
- A luxurious, high-quality turtleneck
- Classic solid black or white swimwear
- A seasonably and location appropriate tote
- Cocktail dress in a solid, neutral color
- Evening shoes and clutch to compliment selected cocktail dress
- Walk-friendly pointed toe pumps and complimenting top handle bag
- Flats, elegant sandals, and white classic tennis shoes
- A seasonably appropriate boater hat and beret
- A classic trench coat (for rainy or cooler destinations)

The art of travel extends far beyond clothing. It's about the way you interact with people, your posture, your demeanor, and your ability to adapt to unfamiliar surroundings. A gentle smile, a kind word, and a genuine interest in the local culture can go a long way in creating a positive and memorable experience. Practice active listening, asking thoughtful questions, and engaging in respectful dialogue. Be mindful of your surroundings, whether it's a crowded market, a serene temple, or a bustling restaurant. Let your curiosity guide you, but always approach with humility and respect.

Traveling offers the opportunity to expand your horizons, to learn about new customs, and to appreciate the diversity of human experiences. It's a chance to step outside your comfort zone, to challenge your perspectives, and to gain a deeper understanding of the world around you. Embrace the unknown with an open mind, a willingness to learn, and a genuine desire to connect with others. Seek out local experiences, sample regional cuisine, and engage in conversations with people who are different from you. These interactions, when approached with grace and respect, can be some of the most enriching moments of your journey.

Think of elegance as a compass, guiding you through the complexities of travel, reminding you of the importance of respect, mindfulness, and cultural sensitivity. Embrace the journey with a sense of purpose and a desire to experience the world with an open heart. Let elegance become your passport to a more fulfilling and meaningful travel experience, enriching not only your own journey but also the lives of those you encounter along the way.

As you navigate different landscapes, embrace local traditions, and engage in meaningful conversations, your elegance will evolve. It will become more nuanced, more authentic, and more reflective of your personal experiences. The lessons learned during your travels will shape your understanding of elegance, enriching your appreciation for its enduring power.

Ultimately, elegance in travel is about finding a balance between personal style and cultural respect, embracing the journey with grace and mindfulness, and allowing your experiences to enrich your perspective on the world. It's a reminder that elegance isn't confined to a particular place or time; it's a way of being . . . a mindset that can guide you through every adventure.

Embracing the Unexpected

Life is a complex journey, filled with moments of happiness, sadness, success, and challenges. Despite our efforts to maintain structure and stability, the unexpected can throw us off course, leaving us feeling lost. However, these disruptions also offer a chance to uncover a hidden strength and grace that rises from our shattered expectations.

Imagine yourself walking down a bustling city street, a symphony of sights and sounds swirling around you. Suddenly, a gust of wind whips around, sending your expensive blowout into disarray and scattering the contents of your purse across the pavement. It's an unexpected challenge, a moment that could easily throw you off balance. But how you respond in that instant reveals a deeper truth about your inner elegance.

Do you succumb to chaos, frustration, and resentment? Or do you maintain composure and face the situation with grace? Do you let the wind control your emotions, or do you find beauty in the midst of disarray?

True elegance is staying calm and adapting gracefully when faced with unexpected challenges. It's also about finding purpose during difficult times and recognizing that challenges make us stronger and reveal our inner strength.

Imagine a willow tree, gracefully swaying in the breeze. Its flexible branches never snap, but rather bend and flow with the wind. This adaptability is a symbol of elegance. In difficult situations, we can take inspiration from the willow's wisdom and learn to adjust and find a new way forward without losing our balance.

To find elegance in life's challenges, consider these practical tips:

Cultivate a Positive Attitude

Our thoughts shape our reality. When faced with unexpected circumstances, choosing to focus on the positive aspects, even amidst the difficulties, can shift our perspective and help us find creative solutions. It's about reframing challenges as opportunities for growth, learning, and resilience.

Embrace Flexibility

Life rarely unfolds according to our plans. Cultivating flexibility, a willingness to adapt and adjust, allows us to navigate life's unexpected turns with grace. It's about releasing the need for control, embracing the unknown, and finding beauty in the spontaneity of life.

Practice Patience

Unexpected challenges often test our patience. By practicing patience, we can navigate difficulties with a calmer demeanor, allowing ourselves the time and space to respond with wisdom and compassion rather than impulsivity or frustration.

Seek Support

When faced with overwhelming challenges, reaching out to loved ones, mentors, or professionals for support can provide opportunities for growth and transformation.

Embracing the unexpected means accepting that life isn't always easy or pleasant. It's acknowledging that life is unpredictable, and challenges will arise. How we handle these challenges shapes our experiences and defines who we are. It's finding peace in chaos, strength during tough times, and purpose in unexpected twists and turns. This is where the true beauty of life lies – not in external appearances, but in our inner resilience and strength.

Elegance is not a fixed state, but a constantly evolving process of self-discovery and improvement. It combines grace, strength, and optimism, reflecting the inner beauty within us. As we face life's challenges, let us remember that elegance is a journey, guided by poise, grace and a firm belief in the beauty of life.

As this chapter illustrates, cultivating an elegant lifestyle involves every aspect of your life. This includes how you approach shopping and the choices you make. In the next chapter we will explore the concept of shopping with elegance.

"To shop elegantly, you must join the brain with the heart."

– Gina Judy

9

ELEGANT SHOPPING

Shopping with elegance is the perfect union of intellect and emotion, where thoughtful decision-making meets a passion for personal style. It's not merely about acquiring possessions, but rather, it's an experience that reflects one's taste and etiquette. In this chapter, we will explore the intricacies of shopping with a sophisticated flair, ensuring that each purchase is an extension of one's refined self.

The act of shopping is often associated with impulsivity, but for the elegant individual, it is a thoughtful and deliberate process. It involves an understanding of one's personal style, an appreciation for quality, and a mindful approach to consumption. From the moment one enters a store, their demeanor should exude a calm confidence. Greeting the staff with a warm smile and a polite inquiry sets the tone for a pleasant shopping experience. Taking the time to browse, feel the fabrics, and appreciate the craftsmanship of each item is essential. It demonstrates a respect for the products and an awareness of one's surroundings.

Elegant shopping is an exercise in restraint and discernment. It is about choosing timeless pieces that will become wardrobe staples or cherished additions to one's home.

Impulse purchases have no place in this world; instead, each selection is made with care, ensuring it aligns with one's aesthetic and values. It is also important to be mindful of one's impact on the environment and to support sustainable practices whenever possible.

Resisting the temptation to buy something in a store or online can be challenging, especially with the allure of attractive displays and marketing strategies. To reduce the risk of purchasing on impulse, determine a budget for your shopping experience and make a list of the items that you need and stick to it. Stay present while shopping. Take a moment to breathe and assess your feelings towards the item before making a decision.

Consider the value and the timelessness of the item. A well-structured designer blazer made of high- quality fabric that fits you beautifully may deserve some consideration, but an ill-fitting pair of trendy block heels in bright green is going to fall short on the "timelessness" scale.

Never buy something just because it is on sale. I purchased a gorgeous classic double breasted, grass green blazer with perfect silver crested buttons once because it fit me perfectly and was on sale. That blazer has hung in my closet now for over 2 years on the unlikely chance that I will ever be inspired to wear it. This is a perfect example of why you should never buy something just because it is on sale.

Like you, I have favorite designers too. But it is important to try new designers. Many new designers prioritize quality and craftsmanship, often creating items with attention to detail and unique materials. This can lead to finding high-quality pieces that are made to last. Exploring new designers exposes you to a wider range of aesthetics, cultural influences, and design philosophies, enriching your fashion experience. By exploring new designers, you open yourself up to a world of creativity and individuality, keeping your classic style up to date and on point. This is how I discovered Kirk Pickersgill for Greta Constantine, Daniela Karnuts for Saafiya, and Jonathan Simkhai of Simkhai.

Personal Shoppers

A personal shopper is a professional who assists individuals in selecting and purchasing clothing, accessories, and other products that align with their individual style. They provide personalized shopping experiences and may offer styling advice and outfit coordination. Whether working with a client in-person or virtually, the personal shopper can assist you in curating a wardrobe, shopping for a special occasion, or tracking down the perfect art piece for your dining room.

Personal shoppers with a focus on fashion may also function as stylists, working with clients to create looks for events, photoshoots, or everyday wear. They often have a strong understanding of current trends and can help clients stay fashionable.

While hiring personal shoppers can be valuable for many individuals, there are drawbacks that make it an undesirable option in some situations.

A personal shopper can significantly reduce the time you spend shopping by curating selections based on your needs, preferences, and budget, allowing you to avoid endless browsing. They often have a background in fashion, retail, or personal styling that allows them to provide expert advice on trends, fits, and styles that suit your body type and preference. Some even have connections in the fashion industry which may give you access to exclusive collections, early releases, or discounts.

Hiring a personal shopper can be expensive so it's important to weigh the cost against the potential benefits. Depending on the personal shopper's approach, there's a risk that they may impose their style preferences on you, leading to a wardrobe that fails to reflect your vision of elegance. There is also a risk of miscommunication. If your preferences and expectations are not clearly communicated, there's a chance items will be selected that do not align with your aesthetics or style.

Luxury Brand Representatives

A luxury brand representative or sales associate is a type of personal shopper dedicated to a brand, a store, or a line of products. Luxury stores understand the importance of creating a personalized shopping experience for their clients. They train their sales associates to act as personal shoppers, getting to know their clients' sizes, style preferences, and even their personalities. By doing so, they foster a unique and intimate relationship that keeps their clients coming back.

These specially developed sales associates are experts in their field, with an extensive knowledge of the brand and the inventory. They can guide you toward the perfect purchase, whether it be a special occasion dress or a new seasonal wardrobe. Their talent lies in their ability to connect with you and truly understand your needs and wishes. They remember the smallest details, ensuring that each client feels valued and understood.

Through developing relationships with these brand representatives, you create your own group of personal shoppers and trusted fashion advisors. Because they keep a meticulous record of your purchases, sizes, and style preferences, they can contact you directly when new inventory arrives that aligns with your taste. You will find yourself on the top of their call list for special events and they may even surprise you with a special gift during the holiday season.

You will find that you don't have to spend a lot to be one of their favorites, but they will appreciate your kindness and loyalty. Treat your brand representatives and sales associates with great kindness. When you text or call them, recognize they may not be working at that time so they may not be getting paid for the time they are spending with you. Avoid asking your sales associates to "set aside" an item for you. If you would like to purchase an item but are not able to come into the store right away, ask if you can pay for the item over the phone and retrieve it at a later time.

Not only will you appreciate this personalized attention, but you may also find yourself eagerly awaiting their recommendations.

Shopping Online

With the rise of e-commerce, many personal shoppers now provide virtual services, helping clients shop online. They may create lookbooks, recommend items from various retailers, or even manage shopping lists.

Online shopping involves purchasing goods or services over the internet through websites or mobile applications. This modern retail method allows anyone to browse, compare, and purchase products and services anywhere with internet access.

Even when you take the lead in your shopping needs, you will find the 24/7 accessibility of shopping and the wide selection of products and services enticing. For the refined, sophisticated woman of today, online shopping can be a double-edged sword. On one hand, it offers an array of benefits that can enhance her lifestyle and fashion choices; on the other, there are potential drawbacks that she must navigate skillfully.

The advantages are undeniable. With a few clicks, you can access a vast selection of retailers and designers from the comfort of your home, or while traveling. This convenience is invaluable for a busy woman, always on the move... you can source unique, high-quality pieces that reflect your personal style and set you apart from the crowd. Online shopping also allows you to compare prices and read reviews, ensuring you get the best value for your money. Discretion is another benefit; you can make purchases privately, without drawing attention or having to discuss your choices with salespeople.

However, you must also be aware of the potential pitfalls. The very convenience of online shopping can lead to impulsive buying, and you must guard against this. It is all too easy to be tempted by attractive websites and clever marketing, so ensure you research items thoroughly and only purchase from reputable sites. Returns and exchanges can also be a challenge, especially with international orders, and you must be prepared for potential issues with sizing and quality. Finally, there is the risk of online fraud and identity theft. Be vigilant about your personal information and only shop on secure websites to minimize this risk.

In conclusion, online shopping is a modern convenience that can benefit a sophisticated woman, provided she approaches it with wisdom and caution. It is a tool that, when used skillfully, can enhance her elegance and unique sense of style.

Always Shop Alone

On your journey toward a more elegant you, keep in mind that your opinion is the one that counts.

While it can be enjoyable to join a friend for lunch in a luxury store's café, reserve shopping dates for those times when you are picking up a preplanned item or you are in the mood to just browse.

Shopping alone can contribute to a more enjoyable and focused experience. Browsing at your own pace offers an opportunity to take your time to explore different options and styles without the influence of friends or family. It's easier to stick to your budget because you are not tempted to splurge on items that aren't part of your budget.

When you shop alone, you can pay attention to your feelings about each item and prioritize your personal style and preferences without worrying about accommodating someone else's taste. Spending time shopping alone can also be a form of self-care, allowing you to connect with your personal style and preferences in a way that can enhance your confidence and sense of identity.

If you are concerned that something may not fit correctly or may be a poor color choice, look in the mirror. Mirrors will tell you the story.

"Learn from the icons but develop your own distinctive style."

– Gina Judy

10

ICONS OF ELEGANCE

Exploring the principles of enduring style and taste through icons celebrated for their elegance is a worthwhile endeavor. It provides abundant inspiration and direction for honing one's personal aesthetic. By examining the perennial grace and refinement of such figures, one can grasp the significance of quality, simplicity, and meticulousness in crafting an elegant and cultivated appearance.

From classic silhouettes to impeccable tailoring, style icons provide a blueprint for achieving a sense of grace and poise in your appearance. By understanding and emulating the principles of elegance demonstrated by these influential figures, you can cultivate a sense of confidence and refinement in your own personal style, ultimately enhancing your overall presence and impact.

Audrey Hepburn

Audrey Hepburn, with her pixie-like features, captivating smile, and effortless grace, became a global icon synonymous with elegance. Her enduring influence transcended the realm of fashion, extending to cinema, philanthropy, and culture, leaving an indelible mark on the world.

Hepburn's rise to fame was not merely a matter of striking beauty; it was her embodiment of elegance that captivated audiences. Her signature style, characterized by a refined simplicity and timeless sophistication, defined a new era of feminine beauty. The little black dress, a cornerstone of her wardrobe, was not just a garment but a symbol of her iconic status. It was her ability to elevate the simplest of outfits with her innate grace that made her totally unique.

Her fashion choices were meticulously curated, highlighting a blend of classic and contemporary elements. Whether it was a Givenchy gown for a red-carpet event, a simple black turtleneck paired with a tailored skirt for everyday wear, or a whimsical ballet-inspired ensemble for a film role, Hepburn consistently exuded an air of elegance. Her signature look, complete with a sleek updo, a touch of red lipstick, and a mischievous glint in her eyes, became a blueprint for generations of fashion enthusiasts.

Her travel style embraced a minimalist aesthetic. When she opted for heels, they were typically low and elegant, allowing her to move comfortably through airports and train stations. She often chose a few key pieces that were well-fitted and flattering, allowing her natural beauty to shine through without excessive embellishment.

But Hepburn's elegance went beyond the realm of fashion. Her graceful demeanor, both on and off-screen, reflected a deep sense of poise and refinement. Her movements were fluid and deliberate, and her voice, soft yet commanding, conveyed a sense of calm assurance. She possessed an inner strength and resilience that shone through her performances, adding an extra layer of depth and sophistication to her persona.

Hepburn's impact on fashion was profound. She championed a style that celebrated femininity without being overtly flashy or ostentatious. Her understated elegance paved the way for a more modern and relatable approach to fashion, one that embraced simplicity, quality, and individual style. Her influence extended beyond the catwalks, inspiring a generation of women to embrace their own unique sense of style.

Beyond her fashion choices, Hepburn's elegance resonated in her personal life and her unwavering commitment to humanitarian causes. She was a passionate advocate for UNICEF, dedicating herself to improving the lives of children around the world. Her grace and compassion shone through her work, inspiring others to embrace a life of service and humanitarianism.

Hepburn's legacy is not confined to the realm of fashion or cinema. She embodies a timeless concept of elegance that encompasses grace, poise, kindness, and a commitment to making a difference in the world. Her enduring influence continues to inspire individuals to cultivate their own sense of style, embrace compassion, and live life with intention and purpose.

Audrey Hepburn's elegance serves as a reminder that true refinement extends beyond outward appearances. It reflects inner qualities such as kindness, grace, and a commitment to making the world a better place. Her legacy continues to inspire us to embrace a life of elegance, both in how we dress and how we interact with the world around us.

Coco Chanel

Coco Chanel, the name itself evokes images of timeless elegance and revolutionary style. She wasn't just a designer; she was a cultural icon, a rebel who challenged the rigid norms of fashion and redefined what it meant for a woman to be stylish. Her journey began in the early 20th century, a time when women's fashion was heavily constrained by corsets and impractical, elaborate gowns. Chanel, with her innate sense of style and a daring vision, dared to break free from these limitations.

She introduced simplicity, practicality, and a sense of freedom to women's clothing. Her iconic little black dress, a testament to her minimalist approach, became a symbol of elegance and sophistication, a garment that transcended trends and resonated with women across generations. Chanel's designs were not just about fashion; they were about empowering women, liberating them from restrictive clothing and allowing them to express their individuality with effortless grace.

Coco's travel style was reflective of her day-to-day style, characterized by her signature elegance, simplicity, and a focus on comfort without sacrificing sophistication. She often selected materials that allowed for ease of movement, such as jerseys, tweed, and lightweight wool. Chanel also understood the importance of layering, especially for travel. She would often wear layers that could be adjusted for different climates, ensuring she remained comfortable while looking chic.

Her influence extended beyond the realm of clothing. She revolutionized women's accessories, too. Chanel's signature tweed suits, with their comfortable yet chic appeal, became synonymous with her name. Her jewelry, with its bold and simple designs, broke away from the traditional, ornate pieces that were prevalent at the time. She also popularized the use of pearls, a symbol of elegance and sophistication, transforming them from formal jewels into everyday accessories.

But Chanel's impact went beyond the tangible. She infused her designs with an attitude, a sense of confidence and independence that resonated deeply with women. She believed that elegance wasn't about following trends or trying to fit into a predetermined mold. It was about being true to oneself, embracing comfort, and exuding a sense of effortless style.

Chanel's story is one of resilience and determination. She was a self-made woman, who rose from humble beginnings to become a fashion empire. She defied societal expectations, broke boundaries, and paved the way for women to express themselves through their clothing. Her influence on modern fashion is undeniable, a testament to her revolutionary vision and her enduring legacy.

Beyond her groundbreaking designs, Chanel was a woman of complex contradictions. She was known for her sharp wit, her independent spirit, and her unconventional lifestyle. Her life was filled with love affairs, scandals, and creative triumphs. Her personality was as captivating as her designs, and her life story continues to inspire and fascinate.

Coco Chanel wasn't just a designer; she was a force of nature, a woman who dared to challenge the status quo and redefine elegance for an entire generation. Her impact on the world of fashion is immeasurable, and her timeless designs and revolutionary spirit continue to inspire women to embrace their individuality and express themselves with effortless style. In her words, "Fashion fades, only style remains the same." And that is the true essence of Coco Chanel's enduring legacy.

Grace Kelly

Grace Kelly, a name synonymous with Hollywood glamour and regal grace, ascended to the throne of style with an effortless charm that captivated the world. Born into a wealthy family in Philadelphia, her journey from an aspiring actress to a princess of Monaco is a testament to the enduring power of elegance.

From her early days on the silver screen, Kelly possessed a natural poise and elegance that transcended the artificiality of Hollywood. Her beauty was undeniable, but it was her quiet confidence and refined demeanor that truly set her apart. Her roles, often portraying strong and independent women, resonated with audiences, further cementing her image as a symbol of feminine strength and grace.

In 1956, her life took an unexpected turn when she met Prince Rainier III of Monaco. Their fairytale romance, culminating in a lavish wedding watched by millions around the world, transformed Kelly into a global icon. The wedding dress, a masterpiece of delicate lace and silk, designed by Helen Rose of MGM Studios, became an enduring symbol of bridal elegance, inspiring generations of brides to come.

Her transition from Hollywood star to princess did not diminish her sense of style. Instead, it refined it. She embraced her new role with a regal poise, adapting her wardrobe to the demands of royal life without compromising her personal sense of style. Her signature looks, characterized by classic silhouettes, tailored suits, and simple yet elegant accessories, embodied a timeless sophistication that transcended fleeting trends.

Grace Kelly's elegance extended beyond her attire. It permeated her actions, her speech, and her demeanor. She carried herself with a quiet dignity and a genuine warmth that endeared her to those around her. Her graceful movements, whether walking through a palace or attending a state banquet, exuded an understated elegance that was both captivating and inspiring.

Her influence on fashion is undeniable. She popularized the "Kelly Bag," a timeless classic named in her honor, and her preference for classic pieces, such as tailored dresses and silk scarves, continues to inspire contemporary designers. She redefined elegance for a new era, proving that true style lies not in following trends but in embracing a timeless aesthetic that reflects personal grace and sophistication.

When it came to traveling, she maintained her reputation for sophistication, often opting for outfits that were both practical and chic. She wore beautifully tailored coats when traveling, which added a touch of sophistication to her look. These coats were typically in neutral tones, making them versatile and elegant. Draping a coat over her shoulders added a touch of polish and elegance to any ensemble.

Beyond her contributions to the world of fashion, Grace Kelly embodied a quiet strength and elegance that extended to her personal life. She was a devoted mother and a passionate advocate for various charitable causes, demonstrating that true elegance is not just about appearances but also about inner values and character.

Grace Kelly's legacy extends far beyond her glamorous life and tragic demise. She remains a timeless icon, a symbol of enduring elegance that continues to inspire generations. Her story reminds us that true elegance is not just about outward appearances, but about cultivating a sense of inner grace, refined manners, and a timeless style that reflects the beauty of one's soul.

Jackie Kennedy Onassis

Jackie Kennedy Onassis' refined fashion sense was an inspiration to many women while she served as America's First Lady. Her style of dressing was unique yet classy, and this is what made her stand out. Her fashion choices were always bold and made a statement without trying too hard.

As a celebrated icon of elegance for her sophisticated sense of style, her fashion choices were characterized by clean lines, classic silhouettes, and understated elegance. Her timeless style continues to inspire and influence modern fashion trends.

Known for her impeccable taste and attention to detail, Jackie Kennedy Onassis effortlessly combined high-end designer pieces with more accessible wardrobe staples, creating a look that was both aspirational and relatable.

Jackie's tailored choices were a testament to her discerning taste. She possessed a keen eye for detail and an understanding of how clothing could enhance a woman's persona. Her structured dresses, impeccably crafted by renowned designers like Givenchy and Valentino.

She had a close relationship with the French designer, Hubert de Givenchy. Givenchy created many iconic pieces for her, including the famous pink suit she wore on the day of her husband's assassination. Givenchy's designs for Jackie were characterized by their elegance, simplicity, and impeccable tailoring, reflecting her classic and sophisticated style. Their collaboration played a significant role in shaping Jackie Kennedy Onassis's fashion legacy as a true style icon.

While Jackie was not known to have a close relationship with Valentino Garavani (Valentino), she wore some of his designs on various occasions. Valentino's elegant and luxurious creations were well-suited to Jackie's sophisticated style, and she was often seen wearing his designs at events and public appearances. Valentino's timeless and impeccably tailored pieces complemented Jackie's iconic sense of fashion, further solidifying her status as a style icon.

Jackie did not sacrifice style when traveling. Whether she was wearing a chic dress, a tailored suit, or a sophisticated coat, her travel attire maintained the same refined quality as her everyday style. She was known for her love of hats and often wore elegant hats and oversized sunglasses while traveling.

Jackie's effortless style was not solely limited to fashion. She was a pioneer in the world of interior design, known for her impeccable taste and ability to transform spaces into elegant and inviting environments. Her homes were filled with a mix of antiques and modern pieces, displaying her eclectic and sophisticated style. Jackie's attention to detail was evident in every aspect of her life, from her fashion choices to her home decor.

In addition to her impeccable sense of style, Jackie was also known for her grace and poise. As the First Lady of the United States, she represented the country with elegance and sophistication, becoming a symbol of American culture and values.

Her influence extended far beyond the fashion world, as she used her platform to promote arts and culture, and to advocate for important social causes.

Her influence extended beyond the political arena as she continued to inspire women through her fashion choices even after her husband's presidency. Aside from being a fashion icon, Jackie Kennedy Onassis was also known for her grace and strength during difficult times. She remained poised and composed, even in the face of personal tragedies. Her fortitude in the wake of her husband's assassination and the loss of her son is a testament to her resilience and character. Despite her public image, she remained a fiercely private individual who valued her family more than anything else. Jackie Kennedy Onassis' legacy continues to live on, not just through her iconic fashion sense, but also through her philanthropic efforts and contributions to society. She used her influence on champion causes that were important to her, such as preserving America's historical landmarks and promoting the arts. Her impact on society goes far beyond her fashion choices, and she will always be remembered as a woman of substance, elegance, and grace.

Jackie's legacy continues to inspire and influence generations, making her a timeless and iconic figure in history.

It is undeniable that the world has bid farewell to some of the most renowned icons of elegance. Their departure has left an undeniable void, yet their legacy continues to shine brightly, serving as a testament to their timeless elegance.

As I reflect on their enduring grace, I am reminded of the indelible mark they have left on the world. Their influence extends far beyond their lifetimes, shaping and inspiring the generations that follow. It is as if their elegance has been immortalized, forever frozen in time, a reminder of the beauty and talent they brought to this world. The essence of their elegance lies not only in their physical appearance but also in the way they carried themselves, the way they captivated audiences with their unique charm and talent. It is this intangible quality that sets them apart and ensures their memory lives on, forever etched in the hearts and minds of those who admired them.

Bringing Back Elegance

As these icons have shown, when it comes to elegance, it's not just about appearances. It's about the entire package – the way someone walks, talks, and carries themselves. That's why studying the icons of elegance is crucial for anyone who wants to embrace elegance and bring elegance into their life. By learning from these icons, one can not only improve their outward appearance, but also their inner persona. By understanding the mindset and attitude of these icons, one can learn to cultivate their own sense of elegance and grace. It's not just about replicating their looks, but also embodying their confidence and poise. These icons serve as role models for elegance, showing us the importance of self-presentation and self-confidence.

Moreover, studying these icons goes beyond just fashion and appearances. It allows us to delve into their lives, their fashion choices, and their mannerisms, giving us a glimpse into what made them so iconic. By doing so, we can also gain a deeper appreciation for art, culture, and history. These icons have left a lasting impact on our society, and by studying them, we can also learn about the social and cultural influences that shaped their elegance. In conclusion, studying the icons of elegance not only helps us improve our personal presentation, but also teaches us valuable lessons about confidence, grace, and cultural influences. By incorporating these lessons into our daily lives, we can truly bring back elegance and leave a lasting impact on the world.

"To achieve elegance, focus on keeping the things in your life that exude elegance and remove those that do not." – Gina Judy

11

ACHIEVING ELEGANCE

Elegance is a quality that is often associated with refinement, grace, and sophistication. It is an elusive concept that extends far beyond the clothes that one wears.

Becoming elegant is a process that requires one to be self-aware. In order to achieve elegance, one must first understand who they are and what they want from life. Self-awareness is the key to unlocking one's full potential and becoming the best version of themselves.

One way to cultivate self-awareness is through introspection. Taking time to reflect on one's thoughts, feelings, and actions can help to better understand oneself. Additionally, seeking feedback from others can provide valuable insights into one's strengths and areas for improvement. Another important aspect of becoming elegant is practicing self-care. This includes taking care of one's physical, mental, and emotional well-being. By prioritizing self-care, one can develop a strong sense of self and improve their overall confidence and self-esteem.

Self-Reflection

Mindfulness involves being present and aware of your thoughts, emotions, and sensations in the present moment.

Take time to reflect on your actions, behaviors, and reactions to different situations. Consider why you respond in certain ways and how your actions impact yourself and others. Self-reflection can help you gain insight into your motivations and values.

Self-reflection is not just about analyzing your inner thoughts and emotions, but it also includes taking an objective look at your outward appearance and behavior. This means paying attention to how you present yourself, from your style and posture to your manners and poise. By doing so, you can gain a better understanding of how you come across to others and how your actions may be perceived.

"How do I greet others?" Do I use a friendly tone and make eye contact? What does my greeting say about me?

"Am I polite and considerate in my interactions?" Do I use "please", "thank you", and "excuse me" regularly? How do I respond when someone thanks me?

"How do I handle disagreements or conflicts?" Do I remain calm and respectful, or do I become defensive or dismissive? How could I improve my approach?

"Do I listen actively when others speak?" Am I fully present and engaged, or do I find myself distracted? How do I show that I am listening?

"How do I respond to criticism or feedback?" Do I react defensively, or do I take it as an opportunity to grow? What steps can I take to better accept feedback?

"How do I treat people in service roles? (waitstaff, cashiers, etc.)?" Am I respectful and courteous, regardless of their position? How does this reflect my character?

"Do I maintain appropriate boundaries?" Am I aware of when to share personal information and when to keep it private? How do I respect others' boundaries?

"How do I express gratitude?" Do I regularly express appreciation, and do I do it sincerely? What method do I use to show gratitude? Are these methods perceived by others as elegant?

"What specific features do I like about my appearance?" Identify aspects of your look that you appreciate, such as your smile, hair, or eyes. Identifying the areas that you like helps you to understand those areas of your appearance that you will be comfortable highlighting.

"What specific features do I feel less confident about?" Acknowledging areas where you may feel insecure and how they affect your self-image helps you to understand the areas that you might like to improve. Even small improvements in these areas will boost your overall self-confidence and will elevate your level of elegance.

"How would I describe my personal style?" Think about the clothes, colors, and accessories you typically choose. Does this style reflect how you want to be perceived?

"Am I taking care of my physical health?" Reflect on your diet, exercise, and sleep habits. How do these factors influence your appearance?

"How does my mental health affect how I perceive myself?" Think about how your mood and mental state impacts your self-image and confidence.

"What do my friends and family say about my appearance?" Reflect on compliments or critiques you've received. Are they consistent with your self-perception?

"How do I feel when I receive compliments?" Analyze your reactions to positive feedback. Do you accept it graciously or dismiss it?

"How do I feel when I compare myself to others?" Reflect on your feelings when you compare your appearance to that of friends, celebrities, or influencers. Is it motivating or discouraging?

"What qualities do I admire in others' appearances?" Identify traits in others that you find appealing. Are they qualities you can incorporate into your own style or self-care routine?

"How does my appearance reflect my personality and values?" Consider whether your style and grooming choices align with who you are and what you value.

"What message do I want my appearance to convey to others?" Think about how you want to be perceived. Does your current look align with that message?

"What changes, if any, would I like to make to my appearance?" Identify specific areas you may want to work on.

"What is my typical posture when standing?" Do I stand with my shoulders back, or do I tend to slouch? How does this affect my confidence? Is my posture perceived by others as poised and elegant?

"How do I sit in social and professional settings?" Am I mindful of my posture when seated? Do I sit up straight or lean back? Are my legs crossed? Are my knees together? How does this influence how I am perceived?

"Do I maintain eye contact during conversations?" How comfortable am I with making eye contact? Do I tend to look away, and if so, why?

"How do my gestures complement my communication?" Do I use hand gestures to emphasize points, or do I keep my hands still? Are my hand gestures perceived as elegant by others?

"How do I carry myself in public?" Is my posture perceived as elegant and graceful?

Expand these questions to include concepts discussed in any of the areas of this book or any areas where you would like to present in an elegant manner.

Asking yourself these types of questions provides you with an opportunity to focus on particular areas of examination. This type of self-reflection is especially helpful to identify areas of potential physical and emotional improvement and improvement in your interactions and relationships with others.

Moreover, self-reflection allows you to examine your motivations and values. By taking the time to reflect on your actions and behaviors, you can gain insight into why you respond in certain ways and whether those responses align with your values. This can help you make more intentional decisions and lead a more purposeful life.

Additionally, self-reflection can bring about personal growth as you become more aware of your strengths and weaknesses and work towards improving yourself. Self-reflection is a powerful tool for self-discovery and growth.

By taking the time to reflect on your thoughts, emotions, and actions in the present moment, you can gain a deeper understanding of yourself and how you interact with the world around you. It can lead to greater self-awareness, improved relationships, and a more fulfilling life. So, make self-reflection a regular practice and see the positive impact it can have on your well-being.

Challenges of Self-Reflection

Objective self-reflection and assessment can be challenging because individuals are complex and multifaceted. People may avoid acknowledging flaws or weaknesses to protect their self-esteem. People may also seek out or interpret information that confirms their existing belief about themselves while ignoring evidence to the contrary.

A person's emotional state can also significantly affect how they view themselves. For example, a current state of happiness may lead to a more positive self-assessment than a state of sadness.

For these reasons, and others, objective self-awareness can be challenging,

Seek Feedback from Others

As objective assessment of self can be challenging, another option for self-evaluation is to seek feedback from others.

Ask for feedback from friends, family members, or colleagues about how they perceive you. Their perspectives can provide valuable insights into your strengths, weaknesses, and potential areas of improvement. Understanding blind spots that you may not be aware of helps you gain a more accurate and well-rounded view of yourself.

Understanding how others perceive you can improve your relationships with others. By being aware of how your actions and behaviors impact those around you, you can adjust your communication style, behavior, and interactions to build stronger and more positive relationships.

You may believe your presence and communication style is graceful and elegant, but others may have a different perception. If you desire stepping into a more elegant "you", it's going to be important that you know the areas that require tweaks and adjustment.

In a professional setting, understanding how others perceive you can be crucial for career advancement. By being aware of your reputation and how colleagues, supervisors, and clients perceive you, you can make strategic decisions to enhance your professional image and credibility.

Awareness of how others perceive you can help you communicate more effectively. By understanding how your words and actions are interpreted by others, you can tailor your communication style to ensure your message is received as intended.

Developing an understanding of how others perceive you is a key component of emotional intelligence. It can lead to personal growth, improved relationships, enhanced communication, and increased self-awareness . . . all of which are essential for success and fulfillment in both personal and professional aspects of life.

While it may not be for everyone, I like to keep a journal anytime I am seeking to elevate an area of my life. Keeping a journal helps me process my thoughts and emotions, as well as track patterns I may miss otherwise. Writing down my goals, experiences, reflections, and progress helps me to gain clarity and helps me be accountable to the process.

If it is your intention to refine your wardrobe or improve the quality of your hair, you can record your progress in a diary or journal to see progress and keep things moving forward.

Self-Care

Another important aspect of becoming elegant is practicing self-care. This includes taking care of one's physical, mental, and emotional well-being. By prioritizing self-care, one can develop a strong sense of self and improve their overall confidence and self-esteem.

Be kind and compassionate towards yourself as you explore your thoughts, feelings, and behaviors. Self-awareness involves accepting yourself, flaws, and all.

Schedule regular periods of quiet reflection to check in with yourself and assess how you are feeling physically, emotionally, and mentally.

Keep this book in a place that allows frequent and easy access. This may be on your desk, your nightstand, or in a reading nook in your home.

Invest in a skincare routine that suits your skin type. Regular cleansing, moisturizing, and sun protection can enhance your natural beauty.

Maintain a regular hair care routine, including trims, color touch-ups, and using quality products to keep your hair healthy and stylish.

If you wear makeup, opt for a polished look. Consider scheduling a session with a professional makeup artist or taking a make-up class to learn the techniques that enhance your features.

Spritz your favorite perfume on pulse points like the wrists, neck, and the ears for a lasting impression. Perfume elevates your mood and enhances your elegance.

Engage in regular physical activity that you enjoy, whether it's yoga, dancing, walking, or a gym workout. Exercise and activity promotes not only physical health but also mental well-being.

Focus on a balanced diet rich in whole foods, fruits, vegetables, and hydration. Eating well contributes to your overall appearance and energy levels.

Prioritize sleep and establish a nighttime routine that promotes relaxation. Quality rest is essential for looking and feeling your best.

Practice mindfulness, meditation, or prayer to reduce stress and cultivate a calm, centered mindset. This enhances your overall demeanor and presence.

Keep a journal to reflect on your thoughts and feelings. Writing can help you process emotions and gain clarity about your goals and values.

Practice self-compassion by being kind to yourself. Acknowledge your strengths and allow yourself grace in moments of struggle.

Finally, surround yourself with positive and supportive people who uplift and inspire you. Engage in meaningful conversations and cultivate deep connections.

By incorporating these practices into your daily routine, you can cultivate self-awareness and gain a deeper understanding of yourself, your motivations, and your inner world.

Becoming elegant requires a delicate balance of style, manners, and overall presence. It is an art that involves cultivating a certain level of poise, attention to detail, and a sense of self-assurance.

This requires not only an understanding of one's personal style and how to dress to accentuate one's best features but also an understanding of the importance of good posture, etiquette, and discretion. An elegant wardrobe is more than just a collection of well-made, timeless pieces; it's a reflection of one's personal style and sophistication.

Elegant people understand the importance of investing in quality over quantity, choosing pieces that will stand the test of time. They know that a well-tailored blazer, a silk blouse, or a little black dress can be the foundation of a chic and sophisticated wardrobe. These pieces can be paired with understated jewelry and accessories to create a look that is both timeless and elegant. However, elegance isn't just about physical appearance; it extends to one's behavior and manners as well.

Elegant people are mindful of their body language and the impression they create. They exhibit good posture and impeccable etiquette, choosing their words carefully and avoiding vulgarity or excess. This attention to detail and refinement sets them apart, giving them an air of confidence and sophistication that is truly elegant.

In summary, becoming elegant is not just about appearance, but also about personal growth and development. By cultivating self-awareness and practicing self-care, one can become more refined, graceful, and sophisticated. It is a journey that requires continuous effort and reflection, but the end result is well worth it.

"To be elegant . . . simply step into your vision of elegance."
– Gina Judy

12

AN ELEGANT YOU

Developing Your Vision of Elegance

With a deeper understanding of elegance and a desire to elevate your level of elegance and your quality of life, you are armed with the tools necessary to develop your vision of elegance and step into it.

Developing the vision of how you want to present yourself is a process that requires introspection and reflection. As humans, we are constantly evolving and changing, and it is important to have a clear picture of how you want to present yourself to others.

To develop your vision, begin today by highlighting or tagging the areas of this book that fit your vision. Keep this book in a convenient location and revisit it for inspiration, simply to keep the concept of "elegance" at the forefront of your mind. In addition to a paperback version or hardback version of this book, consider downloading an audio version and listen as you drive or plan an ensemble for the day.

Another powerful tool that can aid you in this process is a vision board. A vision board is a visual representation of your goals, dreams, and aspirations. By creating a vision board, you can visualize your desires and focus your energy on achieving them.

While a "vision board" can be an actual wall display with images that represent your vision, a "vision board" is a concept not isolated to an actual display or board of images.

With the convenience of mobile phones, apps, and other technology, creating a "vision board" can be as simple as saving images on your phone, save content on your Pinterest account, or developing a list of written goals.

Whether you use an actual display or you document your vision in an alternate manner, documenting your vision can serve as a daily reminder of what you want to accomplish and can help you stay motivated and on track.

In today's fast-paced world, it is easy to lose sight of your goals and become caught up in the expectations and opinions of others. However, documenting a visual representation of your vision of elegance is a proven strategy to assist you in keeping your desires at the forefront of your thoughts. As you move through your day, think of your vision, and keep things in your life that reflect that vision – and remove things in your life that do not reflect that vision.

Consider assigning yourself a weekly or monthly challenge related to implementing elegant behaviors, a more elegant wardrobe, or exploring more resources related to elegance. This type of strategy ensures you keep your goal to become more elegant as a top priority. For instance, identify a particular month as a "Fragrance Month" and make a commitment to explore new fragrances throughout the month to identify a potential "signature fragrance." If you already have a signature fragrance, your "Fragrance Month" could include a mindful approach to layering your fragrance or enhancing your signature fragrance with a body oil to enhance longevity.

To create a more elegant you, take control of your own narrative and present yourself in a way that aligns with your vision.

Creating your vision is a powerful tool that will help you confidently navigate your personal and professional journey of elegance.

Let the loudest voice in your head be . . . "I'm elegant."

Once your vision is created . . . step into it. Focus on keeping the things in your life that exude elegance and remove those that do not.

As you begin your day, do you find your mornings are too rushed? Do you have the time you need to complete a skin care regime of cleansing, vitamin C serum, moisturizer, and sunscreen? Are you too rushed to style your hair or complete a polished look with selected makeup items?

Have you set aside enough time to coordinate a sophisticated and polished ensemble for the day?

At this stage of your morning, consider those things that exude elegant living and commit to keep those in your life. Consider those things that are not in synch with your vision of elegant living and commit to change or remove them.

As your day progresses, evaluate it in the same way... consider those things that exude elegant living and commit to keep those in your life.

Consider those things that are not in synch with your vision of elegant living and commit to change or remove them.

Another option of implementing your vision involves conducting this type of evaluation on a weekly or monthly basis. As the week or month progresses, evaluate in the same way… consider those things that exude elegant living and commit to keep those in your life. Consider those things that are not in synch with your vision of elegant living and change or remove them.

The Self-Reinforcing Cycle and Elegance

We introduced the "Self-Reinforcing Cycle" in Chapter 2 and illustrated how this positive feedback loop can be used to amplify any changes you may put in place. Keep in mind, this self-reinforcing cycle works just as effectively for the intangible concept of elegance as it does for a tangible concept like fragrance.

The self-reinforcing cycle applies to all things perceived as elegant, including fashion, lifestyle choices, behaviors, and even social interactions. Implementing any change toward a more elegant you will reinforce that initial change and lead to significant shifts in the same direction.

Here is how this cycle manifests in the context of elegance:

Your Initial Choice

You make a choice to adopt an elegant style, whether it's through your appearance, clothing, accessories, home décor, manners, or even your manner of speaking.

Perception of Elegance

The choice is made with the intention of being perceived as elegant. This can be influenced by your reading of "The Art of Elegance," cultural standards, personal values, or aspirational icons.

Positive Feedback

When others notice and respond positively to the elegant choices you make – through compliments, admiration, or social validation – it reinforces the choices you've made. You feel good about your decision, and you are affirmed in your sense of style and identity.

Increased Confidence

The positive reinforcement boosts your confidence. You may feel more poised, graceful, or self-assured in social settings, which can enhance your overall presence.

Continued Engagement

Feeling good about your elegance, you are likely to continue making choices that align with this identity – whether it's purchasing more elegant clothing, adopting sophisticated behaviors, or curating an elegant lifestyle.

Social Identity

As you engage more with elegance, it becomes part of your social identity. Friends, family, and colleagues may begin to associate you with this elegant persona, further solidifying the cycle.

Exploration and Loyalty

The satisfaction derived from your elegant choices will naturally lead you to explore all things elegant, including experiences that align with this identity. You will develop a sense of loyalty to the concept of "elegance" and begin to notice opportunities to expand the level of elegance in your life.

Reinforcement of Values

Over time, elegance becomes a core value for you, influencing not just your appearance but also your lifestyle, choices, and interactions. This deeper connection to elegance can lead to increased social opportunities and networks, further enhancing your elegant persona and living your best life.

Cycle Continuation

This cycle continues to grow as you experience more situations where your elegance is acknowledged or reinforced, leading to even greater self-assurance and further commitment to your elegant choices.

This self-reinforcing cycle of elegance ensures implementation of any change toward a more elegant you will reinforce that initial change and lead to significant shifts for you in the same direction.

Even small changes you make will compound over time, resulting in remarkable progress. This is the beauty of the self-reinforcing cycle. It produces immediate and long-term benefits.

The 3 Minute Elegance Check

While cultivating elegance takes time, there are immediate things you can do to step into your vision of grace and style today. A few minutes is all it takes to check your appearance, shift to an elegant mindset, and "step into" your vision of elegance.

Perhaps the most important aspect of elegance is your mindset. Ensure your mindset is one of style and grace. Remember to begin by letting the loudest voice in your head be . . . "I'm elegant."

Next, think about your style and appearance. Have you chosen an outfit that makes you feel confident and comfortable? Have you accessorized it with simple yet sophisticated pieces? Does your handbag and shoe selection compliment your outfit? This will not only ensure you look put together but will also help boost your confidence.

Grooming is another key element to achieving an elegant look. Take a minute to assess your appearance. Does your hair and makeup look on point? Does it appear natural, neat, and not too overdone? Does it need a touch up? In terms of grooming, it's important to pay attention to small details such as neat eyebrows and nails. A quick swipe of mascara, a touch of blush, and a hint of lip gloss can go a long way. Remember, less is more when it comes to elegance. This is the time to ensure you have remembered the power of fragrance. A final "spritz" of a subtle yet alluring scent will leave a lasting impression.

As you begin to think about heading out, check your handbag to ensure you have included a mint or bit of lip gloss. Are there any other small details that you need to remember? Is this an event that requires you to bring a hostess gift?

Next, don't forget to put on a smile. Take a moment to relax your facial muscles and smile genuinely. A genuine smile not only makes you look more approachable, but it also radiates confidence and positivity.

Pay attention to your posture. Stand tall with your shoulders back and your head held high. Not only does good posture make you look more elegant, but it also makes you feel more confident.

As you enter the room, take a moment to practice mindfulness. Close your eyes, take a deep breath, and let go of any tension in your body. Relax your shoulders and let your mind focus on being present in the moment.

By doing this, you are allowing yourself to fully experience the elegance that surrounds you. With these simple yet effective tips, you can evaluate your level of "elegance readiness" and step into your vision of elegance in just a few minutes.

By being mindful and present, you are setting the stage for elegance to enter your life. Remember, elegance is not just about the way you dress or the things you own, it's a state of being. It's about how you carry yourself, how you treat others, and how you navigate through life's challenges.

As you come to the end of this book, you have examined and explored techniques for cultivating elegance and incorporating elegance in your life. You have gained valuable information and tools necessary to elevate your life in a way that exudes elegance. By practicing mindfulness and being present, you have taken the first step towards living a more elegant life.

Remember to continue to use these techniques and always strive to bring elegance into everything you do.

"Elegance never loses its allure...

it is timeless."

– Gina Judy

13

ENDINGS AND BEGINNINGS

After several days of walking the streets of Nice, I decided to treat myself to a luxurious hair wash and blowout at an exclusive salon a few blocks from Nice Palais de la Mediterranee Hotel, Le Salon Zen.

Upon entering, I was greeted by a young girl in her early twenties who complimented my style and grace then asked if I had any secrets to share. I couldn't help but smile at her innocence and curiosity. I explained to her that elegance is not something that can be bought, it's a state of mind. It's about carrying yourself with confidence and poise, regardless of what you're wearing. I told her that true elegance is not about expensive clothing, but about being comfortable in your own skin and embracing your individuality. She listened intently, taking mental notes as I spoke.

I explained that even if she didn't consider herself to be graceful, there were simple things she could do to elevate her level of elegance. I began by suggesting that she visualize herself as a person who embodies all of the elegant features she desires. I explained that this technique would allow her to step into her desired vision and become more refined in the process.

As she stepped into her vision, I assured her that she would naturally begin to remove the things that did not fit the picture. This could be anything from clothing choices to mannerisms or even habits. By keeping only those things that fit the polished picture she had created, she would begin to embody the elegance she desired.

I reminded her that this process would not happen overnight, but with consistent practice and dedication, she would see a noticeable change in her level of elegance. I encouraged her to embrace the vision she had created for herself and to trust in her ability to make it a reality. With a smile, she thanked me for the advice and promised to try it. I could see the determination in her eyes, and I knew she was on the path to becoming the elegant person she had always wanted to be.

As I left the salon, I couldn't help but feel a sense of fulfillment. I had not only treated myself to a pampering session, but I had also shared some valuable life lessons with a young girl who was eager to learn. It reminded me that sometimes, the most meaningful interactions can happen in the most unexpected places.

I reflected on the complexities, as well as the simplicity, of the elegant woman.

The Elegant Woman ...

...understands that true elegance comes from within.

...cultivates inner grace. She actively works on being kind, compassionate, and understanding.

...is polite.

...exhibits good manners.

...takes her time in her movements and speech.

...is well-informed and knowledgeable about a variety of topics.

...sits up straight, stands tall, and exhibits good posture.

...is well groomed and maintains good hygiene.

...invests in timeless pieces that do not go out of style.

...dresses appropriately. She chooses clothing that fits well, flatters her body shape, and suits the occasion.

...avoids heavy makeup or overly flashy accessories that can overwhelm their look.

...maintains her shoes.

...accepts compliments gracefully.

...acts as if someone is watching, even if no one is watching.

...is skilled in the art of quiet and silence and uses it when appropriate.

...stays calm under pressure and handles difficult situations with poise and confidence.

...is not a gossip, she has nothing negative to say.

...strives for elegance in everything she does.

…thinks of others and their feelings.

…is flexible and open to new ideas and experiences.

…will take the time to compliment the chef, the hairstylist, the manicurist and recognizes these individuals are artists that deserve to be recognized for the special skills they possess.

…respects the time of others and is never late.

…always looks put together.

…respects others and does not discuss personal information regarding sizes, weight, money, politics, religion, etc.

…exhibits patience.

…carries a travel-size perfume in her handbag for a quick spritz if needed.

…recognizes her time is valuable and does not waste it.

…has a special, unique something about her. She may wear a signature fragrance, have a signature look, or a memorable hair style.

…is quick to express gratitude and appreciation.

…aims to make others feel comfortable around her.

…takes care of her physical and mental well-being.

…walks with confidence and elegance.

...is never underdressed.

...wears clothing that fits and avoids clothing that is too tight or too loose.

...believes elegance is a form of art and she is an artist.

...values quality over quantity.

...does not waste time on social media.

...smiles a natural smile.

As the list continued to grow, I couldn't help but feel a sense of awe and wonder in the enduring charm of elegance. Elegance never loses its allure.

It was in that very moment that I realized the true intricacies and effortless grace of cultivating a life of elegance had become a lost art.

I felt a sense of gratitude to all those who embody elegance in their own unique ways, those who inspire us with their grace, refinement, and the enduring beauty of a life well-lived.

I was struck by the contrast between the complexities and simplicity of living elegantly, and I knew deep within my heart that I had to share my thoughts with others. In that picturesque location, surrounded by the vibrant culture and refined sophistication, I understood the true value and necessity of documenting my reflections for women of all ages. I had accumulated a wealth of knowledge and experiences throughout my lifetime, and I knew that others could benefit from my insights on mastering the art of elegance.

May this book serve as a testament to the timeless power of elegance and its ability to transform the world, one act of kindness, one thoughtful word, one graceful gesture at a time.

"Elegance is not just in knowing what to do, but in asking the right questions that lead you to discover the richness of beauty and grace in every moment."

– Gina Judy

14

ANSWERING YOUR QUESTIONS

Questions can lead to insightful discussions and provide you with valuable lessons on elegance, style, and personal growth. As a final section of this book, I have taken the time to answer some of the questions I have received regarding my journey of elegance.

Can you share a defining moment in your life that shaped your sense of style or elegance?

Thinking over my life I believe I have likely had thousands of defining moments. Each moment served to educate me on the things that did and did not work with my size, coloring, hair, and personal brand.

For example, photographs of my attempts to wear a bold chartreuse dress to a holiday party or a floral print dress to a wedding ensured I understood that straying from solid classic colors would likely end in a disastrous silhouette on my smaller frame. While these moments do not represent a single defining moment, collectively they have served to educate me on the colors and patterns that do not compliment me.

These moments also occur each time I slip on a beautifully tailored blazer in a color that flatters my features, or I carry a luxury handbag with an exquisite locking structure. In these moments I feel and look like the elegant woman in my vision.

So perhaps the lesson to learn here is that the elegant woman has likely experienced defining moments occurring throughout their life. Elevating your style and grace comes from experiencing these moments with objective self-awareness and a desire to improve.

How do you incorporate current trends while staying true to your personal style?

Over time I have learned that it is much easier to incorporate a single trendy accessory than trying to pull off an entire outfit. Trendy accessories, like statement jewelry, scarves, or handbags can be incorporated with classic outfits to keep your look up-to-date. Adding a trendy Prada crossbody or wearing a padded Prada headband to a structured black mini dress can elevate a classic look. Trendy sunglasses are another way to keep on-trend.

Trendy clothing can be more challenging, but staying with solid colors and simple designs will provide you with a fairly clean piece with which you can work. For instance, trendy high-waisted jeans can be paired with a classic black turtleneck, black pumps, and a structured black top handle bag. As long as you keep your jewelry simple and sophisticated, you will be pleased with the fashion forward end-result of this ensemble.

I understand that not every trend will suit my size, complexion, hair color or hair length. As a result, I attempt to minimize trendy pieces to ones that resonate with my personal style, and I make adjustments to ensure they fit seamlessly with my classic aesthetic. For example, adding a trendy oversized Prada headband and the Prada Saffiano triangle crossbody shifts the Sportmax Tefrite mini dress from a classic look to a fashion forward silhouette.

Overall, I find that incorporating small trendy touches into a classic style can create a fresh and youthful vibe while maintaining a sense of timeless elegance.

Can you share a memorable experience where elegance made a significant impact?

While there have been a number of experiences where elegance made a significant impact, the one that is most memorable is my wedding day in October of 2023.

The day unfolded like a dream, marked by an air of elegance that I believe resonated deeply with our guests and left an enduring impression. Set against a beautiful desert mountain backdrop, every detail was thoughtfully curated to reflect our love story – from the crystal arrangements to the talented musicians that filled the air with classic love songs. The sparkling, enchanting atmosphere created a sense of intimacy that enveloped everyone present.

Guests later shared how the elegance of the day inspired them, sparking conversations about love, commitment, and the beauty of celebrating life's significant moments. It was a reminder that elegance is not just about aesthetics but also about the connections we forge and the memories we create together.

How do you choose outfits for different occasions?

To choose an outfit for a certain occasion, I begin planning as soon as possible. Understanding the event's formality, location, and dress code is one of my first considerations. Next, I consider my personal style including the style of my hair for the day. Given the volume and length of my hair, I consider how I will wear my hair for the occasion. Keeping my hair sleek and straight may work well with some looks and full hair with curls may work best with other outfits.

Staying true to my personal style, I select an ensemble and move it to a clothing bar in my closet then proceed to accessorize it with a pair of shoes and handbag. With these pieces together, I consider whether a hat, scarf, statement jewelry, or coat might be appropriate for the occasion. I add accessories to the ensemble, step back to look at the overall visual, and then ask myself, "Is this the image I want to project?"

For special events, I may select two ensembles and make a final decision closer to the date of the event.

How do you handle criticism or haters?

Primarily, I try not to react. Engaging with negativity can drain your emotional and mental resources. By choosing to ignore haters, you preserve your energy for more constructive pursuits and positive relationships that uplift you. Haters often thrive on negativity and conflict. By ignoring them, you redirect your focus toward positivity, allowing you to cultivate a more optimistic mindset. Simply stated, don't give haters the time or energy.

Keep ascending and don't let haters distract you. Remember, their negativity is more about them than it is you.

What are some key elements of your daily routine that contribute to your sense of elegance?

I make my bed. This may sound like a small act, but it is an act that has a major impact in my life. Starting the day by making my bed sets a positive tone and establishes a productive routine. It is a signal for my mind that I am ready to tackle my day with positivity and provides me with a few moments to begin my day with intention and with an elegant mindset. A neatly made bed also transforms my bedroom into a serene sanctuary, creating a visually appealing and inviting space. It enhances my mood and makes it easier to feel composed and elegant throughout the day.

The habit of making my bed inspires me to approach other aspects of my life with the same level of care and intention.

I value self-awareness and improvement. Whether it is spending a few minutes in prayer or reflection each day, writing, or noting accomplishments, self-awareness is a critical part of my personal development and emotional intelligence. By understanding my strengths and areas for improvement, I can set meaningful goals and work toward becoming the best version of myself.

Just like I take the time to practice good personal hygiene habits each morning, I take the time to plan what I will wear for the day. Taking the time to plan my outfits helps me organize my wardrobe and make better use of my clothing. I have found that a little planning ensures I have appropriate outfits for various activities and sets a positive tone for the day.

What are some of your favorite ways to express your personality through fashion?

While I tend to stay away from low-quality fabrics that sparkle and shine, I love high-quality fabrics with a touch of glamour. One of my favorite cocktail event looks is a structured blazer dress with a bit of crystal embellishment. Whether it is a Simkhai blazer with an intricate rhinestone chandelier design or a tweed blazer shorts-suit with a couple of rhinestone buttons, a touch of glitz allows me to exhibit a little glamour on occasion.

I am also a huge fan of a well-structured hat to complete an ensemble. A solid black Dior or Gigi Burris beret is perfect with a houndstooth blazer dress, black Dior pumps, and a Lady Dior black bag with silver charms. A navy Maison Michel beret with a double-breasted navy dress and a navy Louis Vuitton bag with bold silver jewelry is a sharp, sophisticated look to attend church on a Sunday morning.

How do you maintain poise and grace in challenging situations?

While maintaining poise and grace in challenging situations depends a lot on the situation, generally speaking it requires a blend of self-awareness, emotional regulation, and effective communication. Ultimately, grace under pressure is about embodying a sense of resilience and dignity. The key is to navigate the difficulty with a calm and composed demeanor.

This might begin with taking a deep breath. This moment of pause tends to help calm my nerves and clear my mind. I try to focus on the present moment rather than the outcome.

Unless someone is using abusive language or treating me with rudeness, I try to actively listen to show respect for them. Taking time to actively listen also allows time to respond thoughtfully instead of reactively. If the situation includes any signs of abusive treatment, I will cease the conversation and remove myself from the situation. No one has the right to speak abusively to you. It is always more elegant to remove yourself from mean, hateful remarks, and unkind people.

What role does self-care play in maintaining your elegance?

When I feel good about how I look, it reflects in my confidence and poise, key components of elegance. I maintain a self-care regime that includes an emphasis on positive energy, physical appearance, physical health, and mental well-being. Taking time for self-care allows me to recharge and return to responsibilities with energy and creativity. It also allows me to feel balanced, fulfilled, and better equipped to engage positively with others. Routine self-care helps me to recognize the importance of rest, improves my mood, and contributes to my overall happiness.

Self-care also helps me maintain a mindset of self-compassion. Recognizing the importance of caring leads me to have a greater acceptance of my flaws and challenges. In turn, this promotes emotional healing and growth.

Any final thoughts for someone dedicated to the pursuit of a more elegant life?

I intentionally designed this book to be small enough to carry and easy to access. Its compact size makes it the perfect companion for your daily commute or a last-minute read before bed. The timeless design adds a touch of sophistication to any space and serves as a constant reminder to embrace elegance in all aspects of your life. This simple design will look lovely on your desk, nightstand, or coffee table. It's a subtle yet powerful statement that reflects your commitment to living a refined and graceful existence.

As you delve into the insights shared within these pages, remember that elegance is a journey, a personal and transformative experience. It's not just about looking good on the outside, but about cultivating a refined and graceful mindset. It's about making small, thoughtful choices that align with your unique style and values. These choices may seem insignificant, but they have the power to guide you towards a more refined and graceful existence.

This book is not just a manual, but a companion in your journey towards a more elegant life. So don't just read the words on these pages, embrace the process, celebrate your individuality, and confidently take that first step towards a life of elegance. Remember that the journey starts now, and this book is meant to be a constant reminder and guide along the way. Let it inspire you, let it challenge you, and let it help you become the best version of yourself – a version that embodies elegance in every moment. And as you reach the end of this book, know that your journey is far from over, for true elegance is a never-ending pursuit.

GRATITUDE AND RECOGNITION

Writing a book about a topic as timeless and multifaceted as elegance is an undertaking that wouldn't have been possible without the support and guidance of many individuals.

As I close this chapter and reflect on the journey that brought this book to life, I am filled with an overwhelming sense of gratitude.

First and foremost, I am deeply grateful to my mother. This book is a testament to her influence on my love of fashion and style.

I am also grateful to Audrey Hepburn, Gracy Kelly, Coco Chanel and Jackie Kennedy Onassis who provided inspiration and timeless contributions to the world of elegance, which have served as an inspiration and a foundation for this book.

Thank you to many dear friends who have said on countless occasions . . . "You must write a book!" I am grateful for the discussions, the shared dreams, and the moments we've spent together that have sparked countless ideas and fueled my passion.

To my daughters, Frankie and Sammi, and my daughters-in-law, Lauren, Liza, and Katie . . . Your grace, strength, and beauty inspire me daily. May this book be a guide to the art of elegance, a celebration of the extraordinary women you are. May it educate, inspire, and empower you to embrace your unique journeys with confidence and poise.

Finally, I extend my heartfelt gratitude to my husband, Steve, for his unwavering love, encouragement, and understanding during the process of writing this book. Your support has made all the difference.

With Tons of Love,

Gina

FROM THE AUTHOR

Growing up in a small midwestern town, I was raised by a loving family with strong Christian values. As I matured, I realized the importance of these values and how they would shape me into the person I would become. Despite the limitations of living in a small town, I desired a life beyond my humble beginnings. Like many other girls of that time, my parents encouraged good manners, kindness, and doing your "very best" in everything. They also recognized an interest in beauty, fashion, and style which they encouraged me to develop.

It was from these humble beginnings that my love of etiquette, fashion, and poise was rooted and grew. As I grew older, my passion and interest in learning more about elegance, style, and grace never faded. It was a way for me to express myself in a way that I felt was my "very best".

Now, whether I am in the comfort of my own home or attending high-profile events, I feel at ease in any setting. My knowledge and understanding of etiquette and style has not only helped me feel more confident, but it has opened doors and allowed me to navigate social situations with ease. I am constantly learning and evolving, but my foundation in these areas has given me a solid framework to build upon. I am a firm believer that the way we present ourselves to the world reflects who we are. I am proud to say that my interest in etiquette, style, and grace has not wavered over the years.

It has allowed me to express myself in a way that feels authentic and true to who I am.

It has become a part of my identity, and I am grateful for how it has positively impacted my life.

My understanding of elegance has helped me become the best version of myself and I believe it can do the same for you.

Enjoy your journey!

Gina